UNDERSTANDING
EUDORA WELTY

Understanding Contemporary American Literature

Matthew J. Bruccoli, Series Editor

Volumes on

UNDERSTANDING
EUDORA
WELTY

Michael Kreyling

University of South Carolina Press

Published in Columbia, South Carolina, by the
University of South Carolina Press

Manufactured in the United States of America

03 02 01 00 99   5 4 3 2 1

Library of Congress Cataloging-in-Publication Data

Kreyling, Michael, 1948–
  Understanding Eudora Welty / Michael Kreyling.
    p. cm. — (Understanding contemporary American literature)
  Includes bibliographical references (p.) and index.
  ISBN 1-57003-283-1
  1. Welty, Eudora, 1909– —Criticism and interpretation.
  2. Women and literature—Southern States—History—
  20th century. I. Title. II. Series.
  PS3545.E6 Z752 1999
  813'.52—dc21   98-40292

To Eudora Welty, with thanks

CONTENTS

EDITOR'S PREFACE

The volumes of the Understanding Contemporary American Literature (UCAL) series have been planned as guides or companions for students as well as nonacademic readers. The editor and publisher perceive a need for these volumes because much influential contemporary literature makes special demands. Uninitiated readers encounter difficulty in approaching works that depart from the traditional forms and techniques of prose and poetry. Literature relies on conventions, but the conventions keep evolving; new writers form their own conventions—which in time may become familiar. Put simply, UCAL provides instruction in how to read certain contemporary writers—identifying and explicating their material, themes, use of language, point of view, structures, symbolism, and responses to experience.

The word understanding in the titles was deliberately chosen. Many willing readers lack an adequate understanding of how contemporary literature works; that is, what the author is attempting to express and the means by which it is conveyed. Although the criticism and analysis in the series have been aimed at a level of general accessibility, these introductory volumes are meant to be applied in conjunction with the works they cover. They do not provide a substitute for the works and authors they introduce, but rather prepare the reader for more profitable literary experiences.

M.J.B.

Introduction

Eudora Alice Welty was born in Jackson, Mississippi, April 13, 1909. Her father was Christian Webb Welty, an Ohioan who had moved to the capital city of Mississippi just after the turn of the century to work for Lamar Life Insurance Company. By the time of his death from leukemia at age fifty-two in 1931, Christian Welty had risen to the position of president, entrusted along the way with such important corporate projects as the design and construction of the company headquarters, a ten-story "skyscraper" in downtown Jackson across Capitol Street from the governor's residence. Welty's mother, Chestina Andrews Welty (1883–1966), who as a young West Virginian taught in a rural school, survived her husband by almost forty years. Welty's prose portraits of Becky Thurston McKelva in *The Optimist's Daughter* (1969 and 1972) and of Mrs. Welty herself in *One Writer's Beginnings* (1983) reflect the major traits of her mother's character. Situations involving family interrelationships, especially between mothers and daughters, are prominent in Welty's fiction and provide one "master theme" for ordering many of her diverse works.

Eudora Welty was educated in the Jackson public schools. Reading and being read to at home shaped a literary temperament and imagination early in her life. Welty has written wryly in *One Writer's Beginnings* of trips to the public library to get books well beyond the "normal" range for a girl her age, and of negotiating with her mother and the librarian to keep her reading horizon expanding. Her early reading was, not surprisingly, omnivorous: Grimm's fairy tales, Greek and Roman mythology, histories of opera and music, encyclopedias of useful and arcane information, and a raft of popular and literary titles more or less available in a medium-sized southern town before the First World War. Advanced reading came in high school and college. Welty attended Central High School in Jackson. Her writing career can be said to begin here, with contributions to *Hi-Lite,* the high-school paper, and farther afield to *St. Nicholas Magazine,* a youth publication that ran the gamut from elementary-school readers to adolescents.

From 1925 to 1927 Welty attended Mississippi State College for Women about 150 miles northeast of Jackson, in Columbus, Mississippi. For *The Spectator,* the campus newspaper, Welty wrote humorous squibs, sketches, and poems. In 1927, Welty went north to the University of Wisconsin, where she earned a B.A. in 1929. In Madison, the young woman found a literary, artistic, and cultural milieu commensurate with her ambition. In formal memoirs and in letters, Welty remembers her two years at the University of Wisconsin as an initiation into a mature literary life. Her classes introduced her to the full roster of canonical Western literature and solidified her admiration for the work of living contemporaries, especially W. B. Yeats. Madison, Wisconsin, did not forget the former student. When her first book, *A Curtain of Green and Other Stories,* was published in 1941, August Derleth praised it in the *Madison Times* (7 December 1941), reminding his readers that there was a definite connection between Welty's UW degree and the quality of her fiction.

Traveling by train between Madison and Jackson also contributed to the shaping of the writer's imagination. The journey motif, another "master theme" so prominent in Welty's fiction across more than forty years, was inscribed in her life early and deeply. In *One Writer's Beginnings* Welty writes of automobile trips with the family, business trips by train with her father, and solo trips to school in Wisconsin and, later, to New York. Her solo trips were not lonesome, for the emerging writer's attention was always alert to the possibilities for stories in the people she met and the things she saw. For example, long layovers in Chicago between the arrival of the train from Mississippi and the departure of the train to Madison brought Welty into closer contact with the world of modern painting and sculpture. Welty would often spend the dead time between trains in the galleries of the Art Institute of Chicago (only a few blocks from the station), and the impact of the institute's strong collections (especially Impressionism and later modernist works) can be seen in the composition of scene and situation in some of Welty's early stories.

In 1930–31, at the suggestion of her father, Welty enrolled in the Columbia University School of Business in New York City. Although she was leaning toward a life's work in painting or literature or photography rather than a business career, her father thought she should have a "day job," and so Welty went to the big city. Studying the ways of the business world did not consume all of her time in New York City. Welty indulged her love for the stage, from vaudeville on up the cultural ladder, frequented galleries and museums, and made her way to a few of the nightclubs in Harlem. With the Wall Street crash of 1929, however, the mainstream of the U.S. economy had more or less dried up, and Welty left New York and returned to Mississippi when she finished her degree.

The year she returned, her father died. The event as narrated in *One Writer's Beginnings* seems haunted with a sense of inevitability, anguish, and the inescapable guilt that any child feels for a parent's death. Christian Welty's investments and insurance temporarily relieved the family (Welty had two younger brothers) of financial turmoil. Still, Welty, in her early twenties, went to work at an array of jobs: copywriter for the Jackson radio station housed in the building her father built, society correspondent for the *Memphis Commercial Appeal* (no wedding supper, ball, tea, or society powwow went unknown to the outside world), and contributor to local Jackson newspapers.

Major change began when Welty, like thousands of American creative artists, went to work for Mississippi agencies of the Works Progress Administration—the WPA. She toured the state as a junior publicity agent, covering local gatherings and projects that had been facilitated by the WPA. Sometimes she would simply show up with her camera at county fairs and market days. Suzanne Marrs discusses the phases of Welty's career as a photographer in her book *The Welty Collection.* Welty's early photographs were exhibited twice in the 1930s: at the Photographic Galleries in New York City, March 31–April 15, 1936, and at the Camera House gallery, March 6–31, 1937 (Marrs 78). Welty's work as a photographer continues to gain praise. With the publication of *One Time, One Place* (1971) and *Eudora Welty Photographs* (1989), as well as several limited editions of selected prints, Welty has been recognized as a photographer worthy of mention with Walker Evans, Margaret Bourke-White, and Dorothea Lange, three of the primary figures in American documentary photography who were Welty's contemporaries.

In the mid-1930s, when Welty was taking, developing, and printing her own photographs, she conceived of them as forming part of a project that also included prose—short stories mostly, but some nonfiction sketches. Models of such "hybrid" works were plentiful at the time. Margaret Bourke-White and Erskine Caldwell had collaborated on *You Have Seen Their Faces* (1937). Walker Evans and James Agee were already at work on the research that would become *Let Us Now Praise Famous Men* (1941), probably the most famous of the Great Depression–era photo-documentary books. Julia Peterkin (South Carolina novelist and Pulitzer Prize winner) and Doris Ullman had success with *Roll, Jordan, Roll* (1933). Undaunted, or perhaps just naive, Welty assembled a manuscript of prose and photographs which she herself "shopped" to various editorial offices in New York. Her property, called *Black Saturday*, did not catch on with publishers, who tended to think the market for such books already saturated.

If her prose and photographs *together* were unsuccessful, each form separately made headway. In addition to the two exhibitions of her photography, Welty also began to publish short stories in the late 1930s. John Rood, editor and publisher of a "little magazine" called *Manuscript,* published quarterly mostly at his own expense, heard of Welty's work and solicited some short stories. He could not offer money, Rood explained, but he could guarantee exposure. Many of *Manuscript*'s readers, he boasted in a letter to Welty, sat at editorial desks in New York City publishing houses. In March 1936 he accepted two stories. "Death of a Traveling Salesman" was published in the spring 1936 issue and "Magic" appeared in the fall number. In between, *The Tanager,* campus magazine of Grinnell (Iowa) College, published another Welty short story, "The Doll." Neither "The Doll" nor "Magic," nor an earlier third story, "Retreat," published in *River* (home offices in Oxford, Mississippi) were included in Welty's first published volume of short stories, *A Curtain of Green and Other Stories* (1941), nor did Welty resuscitate them for inclusion in *Collected Stories* (1980). Welty's career as a writer of fiction begins with "Death of a Traveling Salesman."

From this beginning, Welty's literary reputation rose steadily and stayed on a high plateau in spite of an output that, by comparison with some other American writers, is modest in quantity. Quantity, therefore, is not the issue in assessing Welty's reputation. By what standard the quality of her work is to be judged is.

Book reviewers, who are the first to sight and name new writers on the horizon, identified Eudora Welty as a southern writer. Her work was compared with Faulkner's, inevitably, and with practitioners of southern gothic (for example, McCullers and Flannery O'Connor). Being compared with William Faulkner early in one's career is an unavoidable burden for the southern writer; Welty has survived it well. As subsequent chapters in this book will show, she has even made some headway in the comparison. Being identified as a southern gothicist has proven a more stubborn label. When anthologists select from Welty's many works such stories as "Why I Live at the P.O." or "Petrified

Man," they allow the reading public to see only one facet of Welty's art—and one that is confined to her earlier work.

Academic critics are divided. There are those for whom Welty as southern writer is enough. These critics generally group Welty with the second generation of "Southern Renaissance" writers, those who followed Warren, Tate, Ransom, and Faulkner. Her status in this generation was confirmed in 1943 when Cleanth Brooks and Robert Penn Warren, who had published several of her short stories in the *Southern Review,* included "Old Mr. Marblehall" and "A Piece of News" in their ubiquitous textbook, *Understanding Fiction.*

Welty's work has appeared in virtually every anthology of fiction and American literature published since then. But which Eudora Welty is chosen? Stories in the southern gothic vein, like those mentioned above, and "Keela, The Outcast Indian Maiden" or "Clytie" perpetuate an early Welty—the somewhat formulaic writer of Katherine Anne Porter's "Introduction" to *A Curtain of Green.* If "A Memory" or "The Winds" or "At the Landing" is the anthologist's choice, Welty is a psychological symbolist whose main territory is the inner life of women. This Welty is compared to Willa Cather, Virginia Woolf, and Katherine Mansfield.

If the longer short stories of *The Golden Apples* were feasible alternatives for inclusion in an anthology, Welty would have the reputation of one of America's foremost modernist writers. These stories, by Welty's own admission some of her favorites, are characterized by intricate weavings of motifs from classical mythology and modernist imagery—the technique made a modernist standard by T. S. Eliot, James Joyce, and others.

With the turn of literary criticism away from New Critical formalist analysis to feminist interests, Welty's reputation has scarcely skipped a beat. Nurtured in the New Critical method by Brooks and Warren's editing at the *Southern Review* in the late 1930s and early 1940s, Welty's earlier work absorbed formalist traits that critics later identified in their analyses. Present all along, however, was a formal and thematic attention to women's situations and consciousness. A new generation of critics trained in the excavation and appreciation of this aspect of literature have made Eudora Welty's achievements in both the novel and the short story, and in late as well as early works, the ground of refreshing, revisioning readings.

Understanding Eudora Welty's fiction can be a rich literary experience. Although some stories may seem familiar by type or genre, Welty never wrote to a formula and never wrote the same story twice. Although later work revisits subject matter and concerns of earlier stories, her vision and literary technique have grown in depth and complexity. Although a certain story or novel might seem to be captured in the work of interpretation and study, in a subsequent reading it shows itself through another facet—all new, full of surprise, always a step ahead.

ONE

A Curtain of Green and Other Stories

Reception of Eudora Welty's early fiction, the seventeen short stories in *A Curtain of Green and Other Stories,* was shaped by many circumstances beyond anyone's control. Published one month before Pearl Harbor, Welty's first book had a rough time gaining notice. Popular literary prejudice against short stories and in favor of the novel also proved to be an obstacle. The same critic, August Derleth, who reminded readers that Welty was an alumna of the University of Wisconsin also pointed out that collections of short stories seldom saw the light of day because of a publishers' axiom that they always lost money. A third obstacle was the stereotype of southern fiction fertilized in the 1930s by the popularity of Erskine Caldwell's grotesques and the pre–Nobel Laureate reputation of William Faulkner as the headmaster of a literary "school of cruelty."[1] Despite meaning well, Katherine Anne Porter fed this stereotype in her introduction to *A Curtain of Green.* Reviewers tended to follow Porter's cues by emphasizing the "grotesque" in Welty's stories. The reviewer for the *Springfield (Massachusetts) Republican* dismissed Welty's stories as mere "groupings into the morbid, without the finding of enough to storm our hearts or enlist our interest."[2]

Welty herself tended to draw back from the extreme verdicts of both Porter and the reviewers. In a letter to Ford Madox

Ford, the English novelist whom Porter had contacted on Welty's behalf in 1938, Welty summarized her early stories more moderately:

> Miss Porter suggested that I give you some notion of what the stories are like. All the people in them live in Mississippi, but that hasn't much to do with it. There are different kinds of people, a traveling salesman, old or silly or afflicted people, a rather paranoid postmistress who has gone to live in the post office, the man and his wife who went to New York and got unemployed, poor people on farms, beauty parlor operators, a little pinhead, a widow going crazy all alone in her garden, a moonshiner, gossips, etc. They are not very exciting stories, although sometimes violent, but only come from the complexity and the burdens of poverty or love or grief I have tried to describe through some incident or moment in people's lives. (I imagine all this would apply to any story at all.)[3]

Self-deprecating about her own achievement, Welty downplays extremes of character and suggests that less pathological themes ("burdens of poverty or love or grief") should be the focus of readerly attention.

After the reviewers had their say, literary critics have attempted to locate a recurrent theme or pattern of images (for example, the onlooking artist figure struggling to shape the messiness of reality; women among flowers and gardens cultivating nature rather than imposing their wills on it) by which a coherent and progressive meaning can be mapped out in *A Cur-*

tain of Green. The motivation is laudable—to find in Welty's first published book the key to all of her subsequent works—but it is probably doomed. Peter Schmidt's excellent study of the short stories, *The Heart of the Story: Eudora Welty's Short Fiction* (1991), takes this approach about as far as it can go effectively. Using the classic study of the woman writer, Sandra Gilbert and Susan Gubar's *The Madwoman in the Attic* (1979), Schmidt finds the central female characters and/or the narrative voices in each of the seventeen stories to be surrogates of the woman writer, and specifically the woman writer in the South, expressing anxiety and guilt for sins against social convention by engaging in the act of writing. Michael Kreyling's earlier study, *Eudora Welty's Achievement of Order* (1980), attempts a more formalistic approach with varying degrees of critical success.

But Welty's early short fiction, the first seventeen stories published in book form, come from several impulses—some tested and discarded, some followed up in Welty's subsequent work—and two impulses tend to win out. These two are manifested in certain aspects of Welty's biography: her early imagining of herself in the gallery of the European modern art tradition (as painter or as student), and her later but still youthful seizing of the unposed, documentary photograph as integral to her vision.

In the former category belong such stories as the title story itself, "A Curtain of Green"; "A Memory"; "The Key"; "A Piece of News"; "The Whistle"; "The Hitch-Hikers"; "Clytie"; "Flowers for Marjorie"; and "Death of a Traveling Salesman." Into the latter the remaining stories of *A Curtain of Green* can go, as well as the introduction by Katherine Anne Porter that has done so much to shape an image of Welty as fundamentally a recorder of southern grotesques rather than an original shaper of words, images, and prose rhythms.

The plan to have an established writer, Porter, supply an introduction to Welty's first published volume of short stories was the brainchild of Welty's literary agent, Diarmuid Russell. He reasoned, quite rightly, that (a) collections of short stories were a hard sell—to publishers as well as to book buyers; (b) collections of short stories by unknown writers were harder still; (c) a published recommendation by a well-known writer, with her name smack in the middle of the dust jacket, couldn't hurt.

What Porter wrote, however, has steered public understanding of Welty in one, not entirely helpful, direction. She preferred Welty's original readers to see the author as a naive genius who toiled very little at her art:

Being the child of her place and time, profiting perhaps without being aware of it by the cluttered experiences, foreign travels, and disorders of the generation immediately preceding her, she will never have to go away and live among the Eskimos or Mexican Indians; she need not follow a war and smell death to feel herself alive: she knows about death already. She shall not need even to live in New York in order to feel that she is having the kind of experience, the sense of "life" proper to a serious author. She gets her right nourishment from the source natural to her—her experience so far has been quite enough for her and of precisely the right kind. She began writing spontaneously when she was a child, being a born

> writer; she continued without any plan for a profession,
> without any particular encouragement, and, as it proved,
> not needing any. For a good number of years she
> believed he was going to be a painter, and painted quite
> earnestly while she wrote without much effort. (CG xiii)

No artist, no athlete, no physician—no person who has worked
hard if obscurely at her or his craft—enjoys being praised as
"born" anything. Porter succeeds in simultaneously introducing
Welty and putting her in her place. She as much as says: There
is no art to Eudora Welty's short stories; she merely becomes
aware of a moment or scene and records it in much the same
unreflective way a photographic negative accepts impressions
of light.

To be sure, Welty herself has often given aid and comfort to
this view by downplaying the range and depth of her own work
and lived experience. In her letter to Ford, quoted above, she
minimizes range and depth. Porter's skewing of the new writer's
accomplishments, however, nails Welty into a corner—the
southern grotesque—and in some quarters Porter's opinion still
holds sway:

> There is nothing in the least vulgar or frustrated in Miss
> Welty's mind [this to scotch any comparisons with Car-
> son McCullers, whom Porter disliked]. She has simply an
> eye and an ear sharp, shrewd, and true as a tuning fork.
> She has given to this little story ["Petrified Man"] all her
> wit and observation, her blistering humor and her just
> cruelty; for she has none of that slack tolerance or senti-

mental tenderness toward symptomatic evils that amounts to criminal collusion between author and character. Her use of this material raises the quite awfully sordid little tale to a level above its natural habitat, and its realism seems almost to have the quality of caricature, as complete realism so often does. . . . Miss Welty's little human monsters are not really caricatures at all, but individuals exactly and clearly presented. (xxi)

Generations of readers, cognizant of Porter's introduction or not, have "known" Welty's work by these features: an ear for distinctive speech and dialogue, an eye for the odd or monstrous, a kind of naive presenter of "complete realism" whose great art it is to give readers what appears on her first glance but escapes theirs.

Some of the early stories do court this kind of judgment. "Lily Daw and the Three Ladies" qualifies for the same indictment Porter delivers upon "Petrified Man"; both are "fine clinical stud[ies] of vulgarity—vulgarity absolute, chemically pure" (xx). The story opens with three small-town ladies—Mrs. Watts, a widow; Mrs. Carson, the Baptist preacher's wife; and Aimee Slocum, the postmistress—conspiring to exile Lily Daw to the Ellisville Institute for the Feeble-Minded of Mississippi. Their justification: Lily is an unprotected, sexually attractive young woman, a version of "Baby Doll" before Tennessee Williams patented the character in his 1956 screenplay: "There she sat, wearing a petticoat for a dress, one of the things Mrs. Carson kept after her about. Her milky-yellow hair streamed down from under a new hat" (8–9). The self-appointed guardians of community order and purity want this disheveled goddess out of harm's way. They resort to bribes to induce Lily to trade in her dreams of marriage for their images of peace and quiet in the asylum:

> "What if I was to give you a pink crepe de Chine brassiere with adjustable shoulder straps?" asked Mrs. Watts grimly.
> "Oh, Etta."
> "Well, she needs it," said Mrs. Watts. "What would they think if she ran all over Ellisville in a petticoat looking like a Fiji?" (13)

The proper ladies' bribes reinforce, indirectly, the view we have of Lily as, on the one had, a fertility goddess, and on the other, a grotesque caricature of sexuality such as Erskine Caldwell made famous in *God's Little Acre* and *Tobacco Road.*

What might be construed as a kind of pastoral farce with slightly bawdy undertones is not quite so simple. Often overlooked in the glare of the caricature is Lily's unfunny past. After her mother died, Lily lived alone with her father who provided nothing for her welfare; the ladies of the town supplied food, clothing, and education (7). They rescued her when "her old father commenced beating her and tried to cut her head off with the butcher knife" (7). If you know where to look, you can still see the scar (9). The strong implication is that the proper ladies fear some further physical or sexual violence, and they want to exile Lily to spare her and themselves.

"Lily Daw and the Three Ladies" teeters on an ironic edge between documentary realism and literary allegory. Which meaning is primary: the need to shortcut potential attack by Lily's murderous father, or the need to offset psychological, paranoid "abuse" inflicted by the three ladies who would send Lily to an asylum rather than allow her a "normal" life? A xylophone player in an itinerant carnival returns on the day of Lily's exile to the asylum to redeem his pledge to marry her, but by then the ladies' seductive descriptions of the pleasures of Ellisville have converted Lily and she wants to go. The train steams off, carrying Lily's irretrievable hope chest, as the ladies change their collective mind and decide to sanction the marriage of Lily and the xylophonist. In the final sentence of the story a straw hat is thrown into the telephone wires and, presumably, hangs there suspended, like the outcome of the story itself. The image of Welty as merely writing what she sees and hears does not dovetail with that of the literary artist who concludes her story with an image of suspense that stands for its unanswered questions.

"Petrified Man" and "Why I Live at the P.O." also qualify as examples, in Porter's terms, of Welty as aficionada of the vulgar and grotesque. Both stories have attracted extensive and repeated interpretation. "Petrified Man" is especially fertile ground. One can start with the ear and eye "realism" of the story, admiring Welty's observation of the crudeness of the women clients of Leota's beauty parlor (and of Leota herself), but perhaps not granting Porter's claim that these women represent vulgarity in "its final subhuman depths" (xx).

"Petrified Man" begins with the sounds of human speech about as far from literary sophistication as it is possible to go:

"Reach in my purse and git me a cigarette without no powder in it if you kin, Mrs. Fletcher, honey," said Leota to her ten o'clock shampoo-and-set customer. "I don't like no perfumed cigarettes." (32)

And it ends with an echoing blast of vulgarity:

Billy Boy stomped through the group of wild-haired ladies and went out the door, but flung back the words, "If you're so smart, why ain't you rich?" (55)

Like Ring Lardner's story "Haircut," which it resembles, "Petrified Man" uses the device of the "candid camera" to surprise a group of human beings in their natural habitat as crude, self-absorbed, and venal. It has been argued, with respect to Welty's story, that she views such human meanness with mercy, whereas another connoisseur of vulgarity—Flannery O'Connor—is quick with damnation. If so, Welty's mercy would have to be very large.

While performing a variety of chemical outrages to the hair of her client, Mrs. Fletcher, Leota tells her news of friends from New Orleans, Mr. and Mrs. Pike (Billy Boy is their offspring). The Pike family boards with Leota and her unemployed husband, Fred. A traveling carnival has come to town, and among the exhibits is the Petrified Man:

"But they got this man, this petrified man, that ever'thing ever since he was nine years old, when it goes through his digestion, see, somehow Mrs. Pike says it goes to his joints and has been turning to stone." (41)

"How'd you like to be married to a guy like that?" Leota asks (42). Her question raises several themes veiled behind the so-called "realism" of the story. None of the women likes being married—to any kind of man. Leota belittles Fred with the epithet "shrimp" (41), thereby calling into public notice his height (5'10") and, by implication, his prestige in the marriage. Mrs. Fletcher is no less insistent in denigrating her husband; she regales the denizens of Leota's with tales in which she makes her husband run absurd errands and concludes by denying that he has anything to do with her pregnancy.

The men get their innings by way of surrogates. Billy Boy has the last word, frustrating the women who, like a coven of Medusas, pursue the boy out of the beauty parlor. The Petrified Man, Mr. Petrie, is exposed by Mrs. Pike, who remembers him from New Orleans, as a rapist wanted for attacking four women in California. Mrs. Pike turns him in and gets the reward: five hundred dollars. The women, however, feel no sense of relief that the rapist has been caught. They are merely jealous that Mrs. Pike has pocketed the reward: "Four women. [Leota muses.] I guess those women didn't have the faintest notion at the time they'd be worth a hunderd an' twenty-five bucks a piece someday to Mrs. Pike" (54). Given statements like Leota's, one can see where Porter got the idea that Welty had focused on unrelieved vulgarity. If all Leota can imagine going on at the time of being raped is a kind of financial tabulation, then she is far down the ladder of sympathy.

"Petrified Man," though, is far more than a gallery of vulgar freaks. Its subtext of sexual politics, enhanced by the classical imagery drawn from the myth of Medusa, gives its "realism" (women's hair, petrified male bodies) a symbolic punch. Well beyond the scope of the documentary photograph, the story grants that heterosexual pairings in which the male is hierarchically entitled to the top position are, in fact, resented by women. Women are portrayed as confined, usually without choice or self-knowledge, into narcissistic physical upkeep that, in the end, renders them as grotesque caricatures of the glamorous objects they aspire to be. Men are no better. Mr. Fletcher and Mr. Mountjoy are servile eunuchs; Fred and Mr. Pike enjoy the company of each other, not their wives. Mr. Petrie, whose every appendage turns to stone, lurks in the story like a reminder of danger. "Petrified Man" skates gracefully over depths of tangled, psychosexual meanings. Welty carries it off, however, as a concerto of voices, each of which rings true. "Petrified Man" reaches beyond and through its "realistic" surface, energizing skeins of imagery and symbolism a "mere" photographic talent could not command.

Katherine Anne Porter reacted strongly against Sister in "Why I Live at the P.O." She found Welty's narrator nothing short of "a terrifying case of dementia praecox" (xx), while Welty herself saw Sister only as a "somewhat paranoid postmistress." Porter's strong aversion to Welty's "monstrous" stories ("P.O.," "Petrified Man," "Old Mr. Marblehall," "Keela, the Outcast Indian Maiden," arguably "Lily Daw and the Three Ladies") effectively groups them. As a group they have in common a strong first-person narrator, figures of physical or sexual "abnormality," sketchy and rapid brushstrokes of composition, and a soupçon of mythological or psychoanalytic imagery. "Why I Live at the P.O." is the masterpiece in the group.

Sister's (she is given no other name by family or narrator) discomfort within her close-knit family in China Grove, Mississippi, has been seen as both humorous and pathetic. Porter would have us lean to the clinical diagnosis. More sympathetic readers, like Ruth Vande Kieft, whose Twayne U.S. Authors Series book on Welty set the early trends of interpretation, see comedy rather than dysfunction, illogic rather than mental illness (Vande Kieft 54–55).

Sister and Stella-Rondo, her younger sister, renew their sororal rivalry when the latter returns home in time for Fourth of July festivities with a child named Shirley-T and no explanation (at least none that satisfies Sister) as to the whereabouts and legal status of the putative sire, Mr. Whitaker, an itinerant photographer with whom Stella-Rondo had eloped. Sister had had designs on Mr. Whitaker herself until, she alleges, Stella-Rondo had made libelous remarks about her anatomy: "Told him I was one-sided. Bigger on one side than the other, which is a deliberate, calculated falsehood: I'm the same" (89).

The sibling rivalry eventually entangles the entire family—a family that in weirdness almost matches the Crummellses of Dickens's *Nicholas Nickleby*. Sister hints that Shirley-T is the "spit-image of Pappa-Daddy" (90), her grandfather. Stella-Rondo, continuing the tradition of the women in "Petrified Man," passively deflects the hint that she has been sexually possessed by a male; Shirley-T might be the fruit of an immaculate conception. Stella-Rondo then turns Pappa-Daddy against Sister by charging that Sister had remarked that the elder gent's beard should be trimmed. This is an invasion of patriarchal—nay, Abramic— privilege that cannot be tolerated. Pappa-Daddy threatens to disinherit Sister and to strip her of the sole status to which she can assert a claim: the position of postmistress of China Grove.

The Fourth of July holiday progresses in accelerating "screwball" pace. Mama sides with Stella-Rondo. Uncle Rondo cavorts on the lawn in a kimono under the influence of some mysterious "prescription" he ingests once a year. He is a "certified pharmacist" and mixes the concoction himself. As a prank he tosses a complete string of firecrackers into Sister's bedroom the morning of the fifth, and "they every one went off. Not one bad one in the string. Anybody else, there'd be one that wouldn't go off" (102).

Sister decides to secede from the family and to remove herself and her possessions to the P.O. There, she has a room of her own and the right of self-determination. The story ends with Sister's relentless repossession of the items in the household to which she asserts title. Her establishment in the P.O. is a republic of one: "I want the world to know I'm happy," she claims as the story fades out (110).

"Why I Live at the P.O." is one of Welty's most popular and widely known stories. It has been frequently anthologized, recorded, and read by Welty for public gatherings. The "screwball" spin to its comic appeal is probably an important factor in its popularity. "Why I Live at the P.O." moves at a dizzy pace, plunges eccentric characters into ever-more-complicated relationships, treats improbable events with everyday aplomb, but does not end happily in a marriage. Sister's secession seems final. Like many a female protagonist in Welty's serious and comic fiction, Sister takes self-sufficiency over marriage.

For all its madcap comedy, "Why I Live at the P.O." is a dark story—if not, as Porter would have it, actually demented. It is dark in its own right and darker still when read in comparison with other works by Welty on the same or a very similar theme: "Clytie," *The Ponder Heart,* "The Bride of the *Innisfallen,*" even *The Optimist's Daughter.*

The visible darkness in "Why I Live at the P.O." emanates from its narrative structure: the daughter of a tightly knit family, wishing for a life outside the cocoon and imagining escape through marriage or work, is continually frustrated by the obtuseness of kin and the internal imperative of her own conscience. After one of several clashes with Stella-Rondo, Sister slams a door behind her but finds no place to go except deeper into psychological debt to the family: "[I] went down and made some green-tomato pickle. Somebody had to do it" (97). Readers well know, as Sister herself knows on some inner level, that no one needs more green tomato pickle, no one will thank her for it, no one will remember her work if and when they eat it. Making green-tomato pickle and thinking that it means something is a symptom of Sister's self-imposed captivity. She is not as "demented" as Porter thought she was, but she is suffering.

Clytie, in a similar familial immurement, will commit suicide in her story. Edna Earle will pretend that the Beulah Hotel is her P.O. in *The Ponder Heart.* Even Laurel McKelva Hand, central character of *The Optimist's Daughter,* is not immune to suspicion that, even though she "escapes" family for a life in

Chicago, the distance between her and the past is no greater than the distance between the home place and the post office in China Grove.

Welty's "southern grotesque" sometimes addresses outer, social conditions rather than inner, psychological ones. "Old Mr. Marblehall" was originally published under the title of "Old Mr. Grenada" and was set in a Mississippi town called Brewster. When Welty changed the title to "Old Mr. Marblehall" she also revised the story's setting, moving it to Natchez. The change of venue released some latent energy in "Old Mr. Grenada." The story, like "Why I Live at the P.O.," is one of Welty's dramatic monologues, narrated by a member of the community in which the eponymous Mr. Marblehall lives. The narrator, however, speaks from an edgy point of view. He or she is fully aware of the stodgy and prim character of polite Natchez society and seems to hope that disclosure of Mr. Marblehall's secret life will explode like a terrorist bomb in the hushed purlieus of pilgrimage and the UDC.

Moving the story from "Brewster," a generic town with no special connotations, to Natchez awakened in "Old Mr. Marblehall" the potential to address southern social conditions and mores. In the earlier version of the story, there is no special meaning to be made of Mr. Grenada's indulgence in a double life. He has one polite society wife and child, and one ruder "other-side-of-the-tracks" household. Moving to Natchez, one of the oldest, formerly one of the richest, then one of the most decayed, and most miscegenational cities in Mississippi (in the entire South) emboldened the hint that Mr. Marblehall's "other" wife and son might not be white. Miscegenation in

"Old Mr. Marblehall" is, indeed, only a hint. Left less to suggestion is the comparative frankness about conjugal sexuality in Mr. Marblehall's two liaisons. The uptown wife represents the bastion of womanly reserve and untouchableness. In a fantasy scene in which the narrator imagines the "other" son spying on the uptown household, the son sees the other wife "standing like a giant, in a long-sleeved gathered nightgown, combing her electric hair and breaking it off each time in the comb" (189). Echoes of the neurasthenic woman in T. S. Eliot's *The Waste Land* and of Medusa resonate clearly. The other son's own mother is drawn at the opposite end of the symbolic spectrum; "like a woodcut of a Bavarian witch, forefinger pointing, with scratches in the air all around her" (186), she comes from folklore, not from highbrow art poetry or classical mythology.

The narrator cannot contain his or her anticipation of the "great explosion of revelations . . . in the future" (191). Like Welty's other "monstrous" stories, "Old Mr. Marblehall" stretches character quickly and effectively toward caricature, exoticizes setting, winds up the tension in the plot inside a Poe-like narrator whose imminent unraveling is always about to occur.

Porter did not like *A Curtain of Green* stories in this vein. She granted the skill in composition but rather preferred stories like "A Memory" over what she saw as "mere" skill:

Let me admit a deeply personal preference for this particular kind of story, where external act and the internal voiceless life of the human imagination almost meet and mingle on the mysterious threshold between dream and waking, one reality refusing to admit or confirm the existence of the other, yet both conspiring toward the same end. (xxi)

The "threshold" story eschews traditional narrative in favor of nonchronological disturbances, conceives of character as psychological rather than physical, and responds more clearly to its status as a work of art by bringing allusion, reference, controlled patterns of imagery, and other aesthetic aspects of the *work* into play in the fashioning of the whole.

"A Memory" is the clearest entry point to the "threshold" story. Cast in the form of memoir, "A Memory" begins with a woman narrator remembering a summer morning in her youth when something definitive but unexpected happened in her psychological growing-up. She remembers lounging on the sand near a small lake in her hometown. The hot, almost shadowless sun (it is near noon) beats down, squeezing vision and consciousness as if in a vise. The girl coaxes a reverie of falling in love with a schoolmate, then reveals that the boy did not actually know he was the object of her attention, much less of her love. The girl's "love" reaches a kind of climax when the boy suffers an unexplained nosebleed in class:

I saw red—vermilion—blood flow over the handkerchief and his square-shaped hand; his nose had begun to bleed. I remember the very moment: several of the older girls laughed at the confusion and distraction; the boy rushed from the room; the teacher spoke sharply in warning. But this small happening which had closed in upon my friend was a tremendous shock to me; it was unforeseen, but at

the same time dreaded; I recognized it, and suddenly I
leaned heavily on my arm and fainted. (150)

In the "threshold" story, the way the story is told is the story
rather than a means to it. In her narrative of memory, the
mature woman corrects her own text, changing "red" to "vermilion"—as red appears in the artist's pigments—and composing the scene as a painter might abstract things themselves into
their component shapes: the boy's hand appears in the artist's
imagination as "square-shaped," as if the hand represented is
first the shape an artist might sketch as underpainting, later to
be erased or covered.

This habit of composition continues as the narrator
remembers her childhood reverie broken by a "family" of
bathers who occupy an adjoining space on the sand. Alerted to
the presence of an artistic, painterly imagination at work in the
memoir, readers are led to see the bathers as issuing not necessarily from a street address, but from the tradition of "bathers"
in Western painting. In terms more specific to Welty's life
experience, these bathers have probably migrated from Seurat,
Cezanne, or Picasso—one or more of the artists whose works
Welty had studied at the University of Wisconsin or had actually seen at the Art Institute of Chicago. Seurat's "Le Grande
Jatte" hangs prominently in the Art Institute.

In fact, "A Memory" makes sense as homage to the kind of
painter Welty might have wished to become, if she had realized
the vocation Porter says she envisioned before she became a
writer. The story is lighted with the shadowless glare of Seurat;
when stationary, the figures in the scene are distributed as Seurat

places his. As they begin to move, however, the bathers become Picasso's property:

> Lying in leglike confusion together were the rest of the group, the man and the two women. The man seemed completely given over to the heat and glare of the sun; his relaxed eyes sometimes squinted with faint amusement over the brilliant water and the hot sand. His arms were flabby and at rest. He lay turned on his side, now and then scooping sand in a loose pile about the legs of the older woman.
>
> She herself stared fixedly at his slow, undeliberate movements, and held her body perfectly still. She was unnaturally white and fatly aware, in a bathing suit which had no relation to the shape of her body. Fat hung upon her upper arms like an arrested earthslide on a hill. With the first motion she might make, I was afraid that she would slide down upon herself into a terrifying heap. Her breasts hung heavy and widening like pears into her bathing suit. (152–53)

What the narrating woman remembers now is shaped by one of Picasso's painterly styles, the rendering of human anatomy in bulbous, rounded, undifferentiated masses. Sexual undercurrents in the scene—the displacement of intercourse, gestation, birth—are held in balance by images from the history of modern art. The man of the bather group eventually takes a handful of sand and pours it "down inside [the woman's] bathing suit between her bulbous descending breasts" (154). "There it hung, brown and shapeless" but expressive, perhaps, of some anxiety of pregnancy (154). Birth comes a few moments later, but not in the aura of joy:

> Once when I looked up, the fat woman was standing opposite the smiling man. She bent over and in a condescending way pulled down the front of her bathing suit, turning it outward, so that the lumps of mashed and folded sand came emptying out. I felt a peak of horror. (156)

The narrator's attention shifts immediately to memories of the innocent, blond boy, object of the girl's remembered love and passion, "unconscious eyes looking beyond me and out the window, solitary and unprotected" (157).

"A Memory" invites readers to forge connections between parallel narratives, the narrative of young love and the narrative of initiation into the physicality of sex and love, death and decay of the body. The narrator hopes to protect herself from the latter, but at the cost of preserving the former in the amber of "a memory." The story does not make a central point about a specific character and her situation, but rather about the process by which the artist, simultaneously pulled to life and pulled away by the passion to represent it, frames chaos in form.

"The Key" is a similar "threshold" story, perhaps less immediately discernible than "A Memory" as carrying the code to its meanings in allusion and visual rhetoric. It is an enigmatic story. Among Welty's earlier works it is one in which she had invested great care and hope, and which very early incurred negative criticism as "obscure."

Albert and Ellie Morgan, a nonhearing, mute couple recently married and on their way to a Niagara Falls honeymoon from Yellow Leaf, Mississippi, await a connecting train in an isolated station. The Morgans slide easily into a scene and milieu redolent of Edward Hopper; they are "nighthawks" married yet isolated:

> Under this prickly light two rows of people sat in silence, their faces stung, their bodies twisted and quietly uncomfortable, expectantly so, in ones and twos, not quite asleep. No one seemed impatient, although the train was late. A little girl lay flung back in her mother's lap as though sleep had struck her with a blow. (56)

Communication is rare in this nighttime world; the Morgans's physical inability to speak or hear is the metaphor for human separateness.

Welty positions herself, as the maker of this story, at a cool modernist distance from the warm emotions of her characters and their plight. She describes Ellie Morgan, the newly wed bride, in cubist terms:

> She must have been about forty years old. One of those black satchel purses hung over her straight, strong wrist. It must have been her savings which were making possible this trip. And to what place? you wondered, for she sat there as tense and solid as a cube, as if to endure some nameless apprehension rising and overflowing within her at the thought of travel. (57)

Or, perhaps the "nameless apprehension" that rises in Ellie like Niagara itself is the fear that the married life of shared body and mind celebrated in wedding and honeymoon might not last another second.

If it is clear to readers positioned to watch but to stay uninvolved, that Albert and Ellie are on a straight track to disillusionment, it is likewise clear to the unnamed "young man" in the station who observes the couple privately. Taking a kind of pity on the pair, this man flicks a room key to the floor, and Albert, seeing it first, snatches it up. A key is, in any context, a symbol of the first order; Welty stakes her artistic credentials by handling this potential cliché with skill.

Like an artist painting them as still life, the young man, identified only as hatless and red haired, watches the silent couple from a distance as the train arrives and departs. Ellie and Albert have not heard the rumbling of the structure, nor has anyone in the room told them that a train, perhaps the one they want, has arrived. Albert has been rapt the entire time in speculations as to the meaning of the key: all of his dreams have been fulfilled in its signification. Ellie has been less willing to hope.

The station manager enters, understands what has happened, and turns his wrath on the victims of fate and disability. The key, then, takes on the meaning of rescue, a place of refuge after events have tripped them up. The honeymoon will be now, not in Niagara Falls; their lives together start without earth-shaking fanfare. The threat of beginning, though, polarizes Albert and Ellie, pushes each back into his- and herself. Albert has already had his private moments of contemplation of the key when Ellie realizes its existence. Now, she wants her free speculation on its meanings:

> Now she sat there as quiet as could be. It was not only hopelessness about the trip. She, too, undoubtedly felt something privately about that key, apart from what she had said or what he [Albert] had told her. He had almost shared it with her—you realized that. He frowned and smiled almost at the same time. There was something— something he could almost remember but not quite— which would let him keep the key always to himself. He knew that, and he would remember it later, when he was alone. (67)

Privately and alone, the couple who perhaps should represent perfect bonding of one with the other begin their honeymoon with tacit pledges of staying apart. The awareness of each that the other enjoys a private or separate meaning in the key self-ishly poisons the honeymoon and the prospects for marriage. Life together goes over the falls to oblivion. Albert takes the key to mean "something else—something which he could have alone, for only himself, in peace, something strange and unlooked for which would come to him" (73).

The key eventually departs the symbolic register, becom-ing simply a key to a local hotel room. But the key will not unlock the future, and the young man who bestowed it on Albert and Ellie—a type of the original couple, Adam and Eve—"despised" the giving of it. "The Key" is a predomi-nantly dark story, visually echoing Edward Hopper's lonely pictures and the film noir mentality with which they are often associated. "The Key," like "A Memory," argues that separateness is the final and perhaps inevitable condition of humans.

"The Hitch-Hikers" and "Death of a Traveling Salesman" further complete the category of the "threshold" story. Tom Harris, the everyman of "The Hitch-Hikers," carries his significance in his name: he is the brother of every Tom, Dick, or Harry. He is a salesman, on the road, and prefers the life of itinerant separateness to one of sociable togetherness. Responding to mere vestiges of human loneliness, he picks up two hitchhikers, one with a sad story and the other with a guitar, and takes them to the next small town. While Harris is booking a room for himself for the night, the hitchhikers attempt to steal his car, and the sad one kills the guitar player by striking him over the head with a bottle. Stranded in the town while the law sorts out the crime, and while the blood of the victim is unsuccessfully cleansed from his backseat, Tom Harris gets involved in a local party. There he meets a girl, Carol, who claims that the two have met. Years ago, Carol insists, she had met Tom when the two had spent summer vacations on the coast. Carol's last name is Thames. The name triggers no response in Tom. He is not Eliot's Fisher King; Carol represents no healing waters; and the waste land is as lonely and infertile at the end of Welty's story as it was at the beginning.

R. J. Bowman, the central character of "Death of a Traveling Salesman," is the estranged wanderer, the prototype in Welty's world of Tom Harris and all loners. He is at the end of his road. This is literally, and figuratively, the scene when the story opens. Recovering from "a long siege of influenza" (231), Bowman drives his Ford over ever-more obscure country roads until it literally goes over the edge of nowhere. He staggers under the weight of his illness and sample cases to a shotgun house, the only sign of human habitation in sight. There he is taken in by a wary woman Bowman initially assumes to be elderly. The woman is seen cleaning a lamp, radiating the meaning of Psyche or one of the wise virgins of the New Testament parable.

Bowman haltingly asks for help with his Ford, and the woman explains that "'Sonny ain't here now'" (237). The name presents no ambiguity to Bowman, for he takes Sonny to be the "older" woman's son. Sonny soon appears in an apotheosis of allusive suggestion:

> Sonny was a big enough man, with his belt slung low about his hips. He looked at least thirty. He had a hot, red face that was yet full of silence. He wore muddy blue pants and an old military coat stained and patched. World War? Bowman wondered. Great God, it was a Confederate coat. On the back of his light hair he had a wide filthy black hat which seemed to insult Bowman's own. He pushed down the dogs from his chest. He was strong, with dignity and heaviness in his way of moving . . . There was a resemblance to his mother. (240–41)

Sonny is an "overdetermined" literary symbol; there are more than enough signals pointing to his meaning. Sonny's obvious masculinity, the low-slung belt suggesting genital energy, his light hair and wide-brimmed hat, his "hot, red face," and his resemblance to the woman Bowman takes to be his mother repeatedly suggest that Sonny is a figure of masculine potency, the opposite of the worn-out loner. His errand to bring fire from his employer, Mr. Redmond, suggests Prometheus. When Sonny boasts somewhat later that the woman is his wife and that she is going to have a baby (251), connotations lead to Vulcan—represented with fire imagery—and to Persephone, allied with her mother, Demeter, as female images of cyclical fertility.

If the multiplicity of meanings in Sonny and the woman might confuse the reader, they swamp Bowman. The relentless suggestions of sexual fertility, of male and female under orders from a life force, exhaust what little resistance Bowman has left after weeks of recuperation. His life reveals itself, in its final, compressed moments, as in fact an arid resistance to life. This is the denouement that lies in wait down the road for Tom Harris of "The Hitch-Hikers."

Katherine Anne Porter's ready dichotomy, "threshold" v. "monstrous" stories, still works for readers new to Welty—and for those who think they know the stories. Not every story in the first volume fits snugly into one or the other category, but readers will profit from trying to make the categories work. It is important to keep in mind, though, that Welty undertook her early stories from a wide range of intentions, designs, and experiments with voice and craft. Long-standing interests in Greek and Roman mythology and the Grimm folktales clearly shape some stories—"A Visit of Charity," for example, which echoes "Little Red Riding Hood." Emerging in most of the early stories, however, is a documentary interest in the sounds and sights of the depression-era rural South running alongside a more personal, erudite, modernist concern with the role and character of the artist in the "waste land." The modernist Welty, like her fellow modernist artists, responded to experience through a complex screen of cultural memory and learning. Deploying the mythological symbolism, and composing scenes with conscious influence borrowed from the walls of galleries and museums, Eudora Welty came upon the American literary scene simultaneously conscious of her time and place in Mississippi, and of the wider transatlantic culture of modernism.

CHAPTER TWO

The Robber Bridegroom

Well before all the short stories in *A Curtain of Green* had been finished and the table of contents set (mid-1941), Welty had written a version of *The Robber Bridegroom* that had proved unwelcome in several visits to magazine editors. During deliberations over the contents of *A Curtain of Green,* Welty, worried, like all authors of first books, that she might not publish another one, wanted "The Robber Bridegroom" downsized to a "tale" included with her other stories. Her literary agent, Diarmuid Russell, who had sold the collection to Doubleday and who was overseeing the arrangement of the contents, argued against including it. Since the tale was considerably longer than the other short stories, he reasoned, including it would throw the collection off balance. Russell was strongly in favor of including the very recent Natchez Trace stories, "Powerhouse" and "A Worn Path," on the grounds that their imminent publication in *Atlantic Monthly* would cultivate public interest in the collection. But even though "The Robber Bridegroom" was a Natchez Trace story too, its differences in tone and subject matter, in the agent's view, ruled it out.

Welty's anxiety over a publication for "The Robber Bridegroom" was short lived. John Woodburn, Welty's editor at Doubleday, had persuaded the publishers to take the novella in order to ensure that Doubleday would also get the short-story writer's second collection. Doubleday purchased the work in the spring of 1942, and *The Robber Bridegroom* was published that fall. Welty's reputation was emerging briskly in the early 1940s on the strength of reviews of *A Curtain of Green* and prizes for her short stories. "Lily Daw and the Three Ladies," "A Curtain of Green," and "The Hitch-Hikers" had been chosen for *The Best Short Stories* of 1938, 1939, and 1940, respectively. O. Henry awards came in 1939 for "Petrified Man" and in 1940 for "A Worn Path." Woodburn was justified in ranking Welty as a "hot" property.

Understanding *The Robber Bridegroom* requires understanding more than its publication history. It is more important to understand the mix of historical fact and whimsical fantasy that Welty sought to combine in one story. Several years after its publication in 1942, Welty and her friend John Robinson, a fellow Mississippian to whom she later dedicated both the short story "The Wide Net" and her first novel, *Delta Wedding,* collaborated (1947–48) on an eventually unsuccessful adaptation of the work from book to screenplay. Welty and Robinson hoped to interest Walt Disney Productions. Since 1940, when *Fantasia* was released, Disney was at the forefront of animation; with *Song of the South* (1946) they pioneered the blending of live action and animation. *The Robber Bridegroom,* then, seems in the author's mind, at least, sometimes cartoonish but always likely to float off the page of history into fantasy. Making use of quickly recognizable folk- and fairy-tale figures, treating scenes of violence and taboo with a breeziness by which some (but not all) maimed or killed bodies are reinflated to walk again, and giving some passages of dialogue a kind of adult hipness that functions as a wink to the reader (viewer), Welty made *The Robber Bridegroom* into a fantasy for adults.

Alfred Uhry's successful adaptation of the story for the musical stage in the late 1970s seems to have realized most of this potential.

While some aspects of *The Robber Bridegroom* embrace the history and legend of the Natchez Territory in the pre–Louisiana Purchase decade of the 1790s, and therefore benefit from some historical knowledge, approaching the story only through history is not necessary or wise. The title is, after all, lifted from the Grimm's folktale, and Welty shores up the folktale lineage with classical myth: the classical story of Cupid and Psyche, for example, informs one scene between the lovers in the tale. The historical wraparound of Natchez territorial history is frankly borrowed from Robert Coates's *The Outlaw Years* (1930), but Welty had many other nonhistorical texts in mind for the echoes of *The Robber Bridegroom.*

The split personality of the book, part history and part fantasy, split reviewers and continues to divide readers and critics. The reviewer for the *Springfield (Massachusetts) Republican,* hardly a mainstream voice, nevertheless struck an important chord. The reviewer found *The Robber Bridegroom* "exquisite" and "delightful." And yet his or her ambivalence surfaced even in the midst of great praise: "Miss Welty uses the magic of metaphor and simile like a lyric poet, and writes with a limpid purity, and exquisite sense of descriptive coloring that gives a warm glow of beauty to a fantastic, and unfortunately sometimes tiresome story."[1] Orville Prescott, later to become a champion of Welty in his *New York Times* reviews, did not like what he read: "*The Robber Bridegroom* seems to me a cul-de-sac, an experiment that did not come off, a failure."[2]

Clement Musgrove is a planter in the backcountry a few days' ride from the Mississippi River landing at Rodney, an "extinct" town since 1876 but prior to that an important landing between Vicksburg to the north and Natchez to the south. The story opens when Clement disembarks at Rodney with the proceeds of the sale of his tobacco in New Orleans. The moment his foot touches land, the weather changes, signaling, like a ponderous soundtrack, impending danger:

> As his foot touched shore, the sun sank into the river the color of blood, and at once a wind sprang up and covered the sky with black, yellow, and green clouds the size of whales, which moved across the face of the moon. The river was covered with foam, and against the landing the boats strained in the waves and strained again. River and bluff gave off alike a leaf-green light, and from the water's edge the red torches lining the Landing-under-the-Hill and climbing the bluff to the town stirred and blew to the left and right. (2)

It is no wonder that Welty imagined Disney animation as a possible form for *The Robber Bridegroom.* She had already created a Technicolor atmosphere.

Clement's first order of business is to find a bed for the night, and according to traditional folk- and fairy-tale narrative structure, the third inn he tries must be the charm. The first two had been managed by suspicious characters with missing ears, the customary punishment for stealing horses on the frontier. The third innkeeper has both his ears, and though they quiver with the nervous intensity of a rabbit's (4–5) when he learns of Clement's gold, Clement pronounces him an honest man. Stopping "only" to consume a dinner of "beef-steak, eggs, bacon, turkey joints, johnnycake, pickled peaches, plum pie, and a bowl of grog," Clement is quickly to bed. "'Pleasant dreams!'" the devious landlord calls out to him (5). The joke is double edged: the clearly larcenous innkeeper may suspect that Clement will not live long enough to have a dream; or, after such a meal what dreams may come to Clement must come from Hieronymous Bosch. Welty cleverly establishes the structural pattern of the narrative—a foundation in folk and fairy tale—and positions the narrative voice on the ironic sidelines, whispering asides and double entendres to a smart audience.

As Clement's search for a room had followed the rule of three, so his occupancy of the room will be governed by threes. Two other guests show up: the first is Mike Fink, the Paul Bunyan of river men, and the second is the handsome gentleman-thief Jamie Lockhart, soon to be unmasked as the robber bridegroom himself.

Clement falls under an obligation to Jamie when the latter saves his life and money. Jamie, with his own plan to separate the fool from his bankroll, thwarts Fink, who has a much cruder plan to kill the sleeping Clement and make away with his gold. As part of his gratitude, Clement tells Jamie the story of his life in the Natchez Territory. He had come from the gentler South, Virginia, with his first wife and their twins. Their emigrant party was captured by the Natchez Indians and tortured. Clement's son was killed before his eyes by being thrown into burning oil; his wife, Amalie, died on the spot. The Natchez killed the other adult male in the party and allowed Clement to leave physically unscathed with his daughter, Rosamond, and the other man's widow, Salome. Traumatic memories, however, leave Clement a melancholy man, one who questions the meaning of accumulating wealth, of clearing more of the virgin forest for tobacco and cotton. Salome, whom he marries out of mistaken pity, is affected in the opposite direction; she becomes Clement's shrewish wife who is never satisfied with any degree of wealth. For Rosamond, she is the wicked stepmother.

Salome is deeply jealous of Rosamond and sends her on herb-gathering expeditions to the farthest and least-protected corners of the plantation hoping for a fatal accident. Rosamond always returns with an apron full of herbs and a story about a hair's-breadth escape. Foiled time and again, Salome becomes even more intent upon the destruction of her stepdaughter. She even hires Goat, a "Goofy" type whose completely literal understanding of language gets him often bollixed up, and gives him orders to kidnap Rosamond and do away with her. He fails.

In the meantime, Rosamond has encountered Jamie Lockhart in the woods, where the gentleman-thief relieves her of every last stitch of her clothing. Like Godiva, Rosamond lowers her golden hair to preserve modesty. Like a modern version of the damsel in distress, however, Rosamond had been sure something like being stripped naked in the woods might happen, so in anticipation she had grown her hair long and brushed it regularly for fullness. When she returns to her parents, Salome greets her naked stepdaughter with a request for the herbs she had sent her to collect. Clement explodes, demanding to know what had happened. Rosamond obliges with the actual truth, which, given Rosamond's penchant for exaggeration, sounds like a tall story. Clement announces his intention to enlist the services of his new friend, Jamie Lockhart, to find the culprit who has dishonored his vulnerable daughter.

But Rosamond finds Lockhart first. Not knowing the gentleman-thief's name, Rosamond is back in the woods hoping to run into the cad who had stripped her the day before. Jamie appears on his red horse, Orion, scoops her up, and rides away like Zeus reenacting the rape of Europa in the Natchez wilderness. This rape seems consensual, for in the modern overlay to the story the damsel knows how to snag her man: "He stopped and laid her on the ground, where, straight below, the river flowed as slow as sand, and robbed her of that which he had left her the day before" (65). Not knowing he has fallen in love, Jamie departs for other conquests under the impression that he is free as a bird.

Far from being afraid of Jamie, Rosamond continues to seek him out. She forsakes stepmother and father and wanders the woods until she finds the robbers' hangout. While they are out marauding she cleans up the lair and, when they return, succeeds in persuading them to keep her on to perform housekeeping chores. Jamie, however, is Rosamond's exclusive target. The two spend each night together after Jamie returns from a rough day of robbing travelers on the Trace. Soon, their passion is so consuming that Jamie skips work during the day and the two spend ecstatic hours in a forest transformed into a bower by their love.

In time, the real world reasserts its biological prerogative, and Rosamond returns home. "Salome looked first at Rosamond's belt and then at her countenance, and was mortified to see no signs of humility in either place" (116). Rosamond is pregnant and unashamed. The comedy of unknown identities prolongs the separation of Rosamond and her lover, as Clement sends Jamie on a mission to find the villain who had insulted a daughter he thinks he has yet to meet. The "mistaken-identity" irony is played out gradually, for Jamie knows Rosamond only too well; it just takes him a while to put name and face together. The lovers are, however, reunited in New Orleans before the final page.

While Welty plays variations on the plots of Shakespearean forest comedy, modern romantic comedy, backwoods farce, and the historical record, she dapples the sunny with the dark. The presence in *The Robber Bridegroom* of the Natchez Indians gives the novella a somber shadow. Jamie starts the counter-theme with a comment to Clement as the latter narrates the harrowing story of his capture by the Natchez and the deaths of his first wife and son. "'This must have been long ago,' said Jamie. 'For they are not so fine now, and cannot do so much to prisoners as that'" (23). Indeed, by 1730 the French had all but eliminated the Natchez.[3] By the turn of the nineteenth century, the present time of the events of *The Robber Bridegroom,* the Natchez were already as exotic as the residents of Atlantis. Adding a background of genocide against which the romantic comedies are played out gives Welty's story the peculiar doubleness that mystified reviewers and still puzzles some readers.

Welty knew of the Natchez from several of the same historical sources that were used in the research and writing of *Mississippi: The WPA Guide to the Magnolia State* (1938; 1988). The Natchez, more than the other nations who inhabited the territory of the lower Mississippi, impressed European visitors and historians with their height (the men averaged six feet in stature), the richness of their "mahogany complexion," and the nobility of their general character. G. F. H. Claiborne, author of an early history of Mississippi, described the local peoples, Natchez included, as "tall, well developed, active, with classic features and intellectual expressions; they were grave, haughty, deliberate and always self-possessed" (*Mississippi* 49). Louisiana historian Charles Gayarré concurred: "There was not a man among them who was either overloaded with flesh, or almost completely deprived of this necessary appendage to the body" (49). To European minds, the Natchez were the Athenians of the indigenous peoples (55).

The image of the Natchez, as filtered through such historians, cannot be discounted in evaluating the theme of *The Robber Bridegroom.* Clement's memories of being tortured by the Natchez impute to them a kind of classical austerity fully at odds with the rough-and-ready behaviors of innkeepers, river men, robbers, and rustic lovers:

"We had to be humiliated and tortured and enjoyed, and finally, with the most precise formality, to be decreed upon. All of them put on their blazing feathers and stood looking us down as if we were little mice." (23)

Utilizing Clement's point of view, Welty captures the punctilious behavior of the Natchez, their lordly "self-possession," even their tall stature, and fends off the nearly irresistible force of the popular stereotype of the out-of-control savage.

The action of *The Robber Bridegroom* takes place well after the armed extermination of the Natchez by the French. The guilt of genocide, however, still hovers over the novella. In one of the interleavings of sun and shadow, fantasy and history, an actual bandit of the historical Trace, "Little" Harpe, the younger of the Harpe brothers who considered the Trace their criminal preserve, moves in with Jamie's gang and begins to take it over. Harpe's cruelty exceeds Jamie's tolerance for gentlemanly violence. Besides, Jamie is absent most of the time with fair Rosamond. In a grotesque but undeniable parody of Jamie's courting of Rosamond, Harpe demands that the gang bring him Jamie's woman. "For a joke," they fetch him a Natchez girl. First, Harpe drugs the innocent girl:

> So the girl fought and screamed, but they [the gang] held the Black Drink to her lips and made her drink it and she fell over like the dead, with her hair and her arms swinging in front of her. (131)

The torture escalates when Harpe dismembers the girl, severing "her wedding finger" from her hand (132). The finger, taking its cue from the Grimm's "Robber Bridegroom," hops into the lap of Rosamond, who is hiding nearby. The imagery of sexual violation culminates when Harpe throws "the girl across the

long table, among the plates and all, where the remains of all
the meals lay where they were left, with the knives and forks
sticking in them, and flung himself upon her before their eyes.
. . . 'You have killed her now,' they said, and it was true: she
was dead" (132).

Rape, other forms of bodily maiming and injury, even violent death are integral to the folktale as an instructive form. Welty,
by positioning Rosamond (the survivor of a "kinder" rape) as the
witness to a more violent one, intensifies disgust with and rejection of Harpe's act and suggests that skepticism of Jamie's actions
is also in order. Thus, the lighter aspects of the story are nudged
toward shadow, but not plunged into it. Furthermore, the rape and
murder of the Natchez girl operate symbolically as the genocide
of her nation. Although there are many "sins" in *The Robber
Bridegroom* (theft, rape, reckless endangerment, kidnaping), it is
the extermination of the Natchez that calls for the moral reckon-
ing that shapes the ending of the story.

Seeking revenge for the murder of the Natchez girl by
Harpe and his accomplices, the remnants of the nation round up
all the white people they can locate. Harpe eludes capture, but
the Natchez scalp the other members of Jamie's gang (159). In
addition, they insist that Rosamond atone for the death of the
Indian girl. Salome, jealous of her stepdaughter to the end,
claims that she, not her stepdaughter, is in fact the fair maiden
the Natchez seek. Salome further seals her fate by blaspheming
the Natchez sun god, and for her crime is made to dance to her
death. Once again, Clement is dismissed in pity. The pity, however, is mutual, for Clement alone among the white characters
of *The Robber Bridegroom* knows historical truth:

"The Indians know their time has come," said Clement.
"They are sure of the future growing smaller always, and
that lets them be infinitely gay and cruel." (21)

A comic resolution completes *The Robber Bridegroom,* although
it is tempered with melancholy. Rosamond is reunited with
Jamie "in time's nick" (181), and their meaningful twins (like the
Romulus and Remus of a new order) are born almost immediately thereafter. Jamie prospers in New Orleans by taking money
in commercial deals rather than at gunpoint in the enchanted forest, and the happy family lives in a palatial home on Lake Pon-
chartrain. Rosamond, though, makes no move to contact
Clement, to reassure him that his daughter is safe and that he has
twin grandchildren to replace his dead son, Rosamond's twin
brother. Father and daughter meet by chance while Clement is in
New Orleans selling a crop. But the new order, in which Jamie
as thief metamorphoses effortlessly into Jamie as successful
merchant, is "the time of cunning" (142) and Clement opts to
have no part in it. "Happily ever after" is diluted by the author's
injection of a strong, but small, dose of pessimism: only those
diminished in moral vision by their own good luck can pretend
that fairy tale coexists with history.

The Robber Bridegroom is not always at the forefront in
critical discussions of Welty's works. Its genre is a problem:
novel? novella? short story? tale? By what standard of form and
performance is the work to be judged? Initial reviews foretold
this division. *The Robber Bridegroom*'s appearance on the scene
in the autumn of 1942, as the ordeal of World War II seemed to
stretch into an uncertain future, also darkened its prospects for

catching on with a wide audience. But, as Alfred Uhry's successful adaptation of the story into a musical attests, a potential for popularity was always there.

Welty's emerging sense of herself as a writer of short stories—but emphatically not of novels—seems to argue that *The Robber Bridegroom* is a long short story, and that understanding it must be keyed to its formal qualities. That Welty seriously considered including it in *A Curtain of Green,* her first collection of short stories, bolsters the choice of short story as its genre. Her handling of character seems to run counter to the psychological realism called for in the traditional novel. Granted, Clement approaches status as a multidimensioned character, but he is the only one in the work—like a film noir character in an animated feature.

Greater returns on critical thinking, however, seem to be promised by examining Welty's creative mixing of forms of representation in *The Robber Bridegroom.* Rosamond invites interpretation in the fantasy order, the unnamed Natchez girl in the historical. Likewise, Jamie is a thief in the enchanted forest; but Little Harpe, taken from territorial history, is Jamie's doppelgänger. Juxtaposition of hard-edged circumstance with whimsical comedy—with the edge kept to a minimum—is a stylistic technique Welty repeatedly works. The relatively thick overlay of borrowing and allusion in *The Robber Bridegroom* is likewise a Welty "fingerprint." Welty emerges as a very literary writer, one whose creative imagination is stocked with reading as experience rather than with reading and experience as two equal but separate sources of subject matter. In *The Robber Bridegroom* she paid genuine homage to the reading that had carried her through childhood and youth. Remembered in adulthood, the echoes of that reading take on a smart, ironic tone.

Only a few months after the publication of *The Robber Bridegroom,* Welty followed her editor to Harcourt, Brace from Doubleday. Harcourt, Brace would be her publishers for the next three decades. They began with *The Wide Net and Other Stories,* Welty's second collection of short stories. The Natchez Trace territory is the vivid "place" of these eight stories, but it is no longer the ground of fantasy. The Trace of *The Wide Ne*t is even more than a line inscribed on a map or an actual space crowded with human history. The Trace of *The Wide Net* is the trace the writer's imagination makes in searching for itself.

CHAPTER THREE

The Wide Net and Other Stories

Welty's early short stories, published in *A Curtain of Green, The Robber Bridegroom,* and *The Wide Net and Other Stories*, should be understood as the work of a developing writer experimenting with a variety of voices and styles, secure in some idioms but not in others, dedicated to the short story as a literary tradition and genre but ambitious to contribute something innovative to its history. Welty's experiments with hard-boiled realism in "Magic" (uncollected) proved to be a road not taken. "Flowers for Marjorie," among the collected stories, continues Welty's experiment with Kafkaesque twists of documentary realism, but it is not an experiment she continued beyond the early stages of her career. The wickedly funny monologues, "Why I Live at the P.O.," "Petrified Man," "Old Mr. Marblehall," are performances Welty found she could turn out with comparative ease. Later in her career she would return to the comic monologue in *The Ponder Heart* and in parts of *Losing Battles.* The "threshold" stories, in which she made use of forms and techniques unique to the short story, provided Welty with her strongest artistic challenge and her deepest creative motivation.

Once *A Curtain of Green* (1941) was published and reviewed, Welty's agent urged her to take on new work that would make her produce better stories. Diarmuid Russell well knew that the New York publishers worked on a "what-have-you-done-for-us-lately" basis, and that to stand still was to fall behind. Welty, fearing perhaps that *A Curtain of Green* would be her first and only book, was anxious to push the next wave of her imagination—especially since it seemed slow in arriving. Then, building on a suggestion of Russell's, Welty came up with the idea of writing a "Mississippi Book," a kind of spin-off of the series of state guides published by the WPA. Welty's Mississippi book would be less a statistical guide to the state than an evocation of its places and history. And the central image for that evocation would be the Natchez Trace. *The Wide Net* was underway.

The Natchez Trace had been of central importance to the history of Mississippi since the late eighteenth century. Covering approximately six hundred miles, from the Cumberland Plateau near Nashville, settled by Americans in the 1790s, to the Mississippi River port of Natchez, second in wealth only to New Orleans in the Louisiana Purchase, the Trace became, at the turn of the nineteenth century, the major overland route for emigrants from the trans-Appalachian and trans-Allegheny east to the new territory of the lower Mississippi. For centuries the general path of the Trace had been a migratory route for animal populations and for the indigenous peoples who hunted them as a way of life: Choctaw, Chickasaw, Natchez. When Hernando de Soto discovered the Mississippi River, he traveled the Trace. The Natchez Trace was entering another phase of its history in the 1930s. In 1934 the Department of the Interior, acting through the National Park Service, surveyed the route of the historic Natchez Trace prior to the construction of a paved road for automobiles that covered the entire distance from Natchez to Nashville.

As a resident of Jackson, a recent employee of the WPA (the agency responsible for much of the grading and construction work on early sections of the roadway in the 1930s), and a gardener who occasionally "poached" the flora of the Trace and transplanted a cultivar or two to her own yard before they were bulldozed, Welty was familiar with the Trace. Recognizing the Trace's potential for fiction, Welty eagerly seized the moment. In 1943 Harcourt, Brace published *The Wide Net,* a collection of eight stories issued from the Natchez Trace inspiration.

"A Worn Path" and "Powerhouse" were Natchez Trace stories that bridged Welty from an earlier technique to new experiments in story writing. "First Love" was the first story deliberately planned with the goal of weaving Natchez Trace history with her own increasingly self-conscious fictional technique.

"First Love" engages the history of the Natchez Trace at a crucial moment just after the turn of the nineteenth century. Expeditions of settlers had been flowing into the Mississippi territory after the Louisiana Purchase, swelling the American population and presenting the young federal government with a problem. Aaron Burr's "conspiracy" to separate the Mississippi (Southwest) territory from the United States serves as Welty's historical donnée, a moment of upheaval and uncertainty swirling around a charismatic figure. Imagination clicks in as Welty extends the theme of upheaval by moving the New Madrid earthquake from 1811 to 1807 in order to couple the Burr conspiracy with a natural metaphor.

In this natural-historical context, Welty places her central character, Joel Mayes. Joel is a young version of Clement Musgrove of *The Robber Bridegroom,* a boy whose only memory of his parents is that they were left behind when the group of which the Mayes family was a part was overtaken on the Trace by a band of Natchez Indians. Joel is among the survivors; his parents are not. The trauma of his experience and the vividness of memory have, apparently, rendered Joel both mute and deaf. As if juggling two balls, nature and history, were not enough, Welty, in quest of a new technique, added a main character who can neither speak nor hear.

An innkeeper in Natchez takes Joel in as a bootblack. There is work and room and food, but no sign of emotional rebirth for Joel. The frigid winter associated with the New Madrid quake functions as an added metaphor for the stilling of Joel's imaginative and emotional activity. Welty pushes her story into the symbolic register where associations multiply.

One night Joel is awakened by the appearance of two strange men, both wrapped in long black capes, seated at the rude table in the lean-to where he sleeps. One of the men passively listens while the other magically connects with Joel's autistic spirit:

> One of the two men lifted his right arm—a tense, yet gentle and easy motion—and made the dark wet cloak fall back. To Joel it was like the first movement he had ever seen, as if the world had been up to that night inanimate. (11)

Readers of Welty's tightly concentrated prose should recognize an early "signature" of her technique. Gesture is of central, if sometimes obscure, importance. The lift of the arm stylizes the ordinary representation of the event, giving it meaning. Welty uses the same gesture of the lifted arm in *The Golden Apples;*

linking it to the gesture of Perseus flaunting the head of Medusa. A simple act is thereby raised above "ordinary" representation. The concentrated scope of the short story makes this technique viable. In the larger sweep of the traditional novel, it might well be lost. Burr (the gesturing stranger) holds no Gorgon's head, but Joel is sparked to renewed life in the frigid winter nonetheless. The stranger becomes the focus of his attention, the reconstruction of his psychological wholeness.

On the margins of Joel's nonhearing, nonspeaking world, the "arrest" and trial of Burr for treason takes place. History falls into place according to the needs of the record; Joel fits events into "plot" by another system of need. He notices broadsides advertising the trial at Jefferson Barracks, just up the Trace from Natchez, but since he cannot hear the testimony at the trial nor the gossip at the inn, he cannot know the "plot" of history. He cannot know, for example, that Burr, sensing the trial going against him, and sensing as well the languishing of his grand design of a new Empire of the West, contemplates flight across the Mississippi. Joel only knows the psychological imperative, that he must not let his connection to this man be severed: he is feeling "first love," the kind of exchanged subjectivity children get from parents. Burr is drawn into the vortex of that need.

As the trial takes place in the noisy realm of history, Joel's love for Burr grows in private silence. On the evening before the trial is to begin, Joel witnesses the harrowing of Burr's soul. Tense to the point of snapping, Burr sleeps fitfully on a puncheon table, a hand flung over the edge. He begins to rave in his nightmare, and Joel, who cannot hear, nevertheless knows that should anyone else intrude, he or she might hear from the accused's lips some form of admission of guilt. Joel is driven by a kind of first passion to touch the object of his love:

> Joel was afraid of these words, and afraid that eaves-droppers might listen to them. Whatever words they were, they were being taken by some force out of his [Burr's] dream. In horror, Joel put out his hand. He could never in his life have laid it across the mouth of Aaron Burr, but he thrust it into Burr's spread-out fingers. The fingers closed and did not yield; the clasp grew so fierce that it hurt his hand, but he saw that the words had stopped. (28)

The physical exchange—suggestive of nuptial vows—stirs "wisdom" (28) and life in Joel, but leaves Burr unwittingly in the dark.

Burr decides to flee. Joel, however, knows that he cannot suffer the loss of love. Gestures communicate the troubling news: returning to the inn, Burr makes a gesture to his partner's wife indicating (to Joel) that the couple might flee to the West. When the woman declines, Burr "lifted his hand once more and a slave led out from the shadows a majestic horse with silver trappings shining in the light of the moon" (33). Burr rides away. Joel follows him along Liberty Road. Overtaken by the posse pursuing Burr, Joel is overtaken as well by repressed memory. He falls to the ground and weeps for his dead parents, "to whom he had not said goodbye" (33). When all else around him is locked in frozen lifelessness, Joel's tears symbolize life returning to him.

Making all of the associations dovetail in "First Love" proved to be one of the most serious challenges in Welty's drive to make a new kind of short story. She mailed off one version to Russell, then had second thoughts. Russell also had reservations about the first typed version of the story, and therefore did not start it on its rounds to editorial offices. Welty was relieved. She wrote to Russell:

> Maybe that was the trouble with the story, everything (for me) carried the burden of being so many things at once. But that trouble, and I hope you will think that I am right, I take as a sign that there is a good story possible.[1]

Welty was deliberately trying to steer through historical obstacles by a map of imaginative associations: her faith in "everything carrying the burden of being so many things at once" sometimes called for her (and her readers) to trust in connections that were not immediately apparent. She did intend the frigid weather, she wrote to Russell, to drive her characters to "an inner intensity."[2] But there were other enticing connections and double duties that were less clearly intentional. The actual Liberty Road did actually lead southwest out of Natchez. Does it also function symbolically as the path to Joel's psychological liberation?

"First Love" raises more questions than it finally answers. The "threshold" stories of the first collection, however, also posed questions of meaning and forestalled declarative answers.

For some readers uncomfortable without hard-edged meanings, Welty's newer fiction bordered on obscurity. Even her trusted friend Russell used the word *obscurity* now and then in suggestions for revision. Reviewers of *The Wide Net* could also be impatient. *Time* found the new stories "perplexing and exasperating."[3] *The New Yorker* granted that Welty was "entitled to her experiments," but preferred "the less labored, less diffuse, and more direct manner of her earlier books."[4]

But Welty, in the new Natchez stories, had left the "direct manner" for good. She sought a technical practice, a craft, for ordering the myriad associations of word to word, image to image, gesture to gesture by which her imagination worked. Pursuing the associations was not necessarily an easy plan. In the midst of the Natchez project she visited Russell in Manhattan on her way to Yaddo in upstate New York, where she had a residency in the summer of 1941. Recent successes in publishing and her first face-to-face meeting with Russell and his family had been more than satisfactory, yet something still weighed upon the writer:

> I came to the top of the building in Radio City and looked down on the sunset before leaving New York—so beautiful—the grand purple mountains in the distance showing—river shining—I think it is about a year ago now that you first happened to write me and it made a change in my life so I had a tender place in my heart for the day when it came around again. It has seemed like a magical year and whatever is ahead, that will keep. Today I've been studying over story notes, and I read all I could on

Johnny Appleseed [a suggestion of Russell's that never sparked Welty's imagination]—then I'll go float on the Finger Lakes hoping that in that nice calm way they will come to something I can do—I must have seemed flighty on this trip—it is all because of a kind of tantalization (is that a word?) over one thing and I am trying to get it straight in my head—Don't worry for fear the product will be impossible and wild, until you see it. Thanks for the good times—It was fine to see you and to get to Katonah [the Westchester town where Russell lived] and see everything coming up and looking that bright new-green—It made two springs. I must have been in a dream awhile ago, I thought a taxi had "Dostoevsky" on it, and it was only "DeSoto Sky View"—[5]

In the new stories, for which Welty had made "notes," she was preparing to lead with imaginative instinct rather than with historical logic. That is, she was willing to trust that reading Dostoyevsky's name in letters that actually spelled the name of an automobile was not a slip *away* from meaning but an initiation *into* it. Writer and agent had, in fact, crossed swords on that issue a few months earlier in an exchange concerning "The Winds."[6] Russell wanted each narrative step accounted for; Welty was more willing to trust the feel of the story rather than its logic. Both Welty and Joel Mayes progress by feeling, sensing words as if for the first, original time.

"A Still Moment" is the only other story of the eight in *The Wide Net* that engages the historical subject matter of the Natchez Trace and territorial Mississippi. Welty invokes narrative license in order to place three historical figures (itinerant Methodist preacher Lorenzo Dow, outlaw James Murrell, and painter John James Audubon) at a certain site on the Trace at the same time. The historical record confirms each man's presence in the Trace country; that each was there when the other two were is a different question. But this "error" is irrelevant to the necessary logic of fiction. "A Still Moment" uses Natchez as history, but the story is not a confirmation of the historical record; rather, it is an extension beyond history into imagination.

"A Still Moment" opens with Lorenzo Dow racing on horseback along the Trace to a revival. Conversion of souls in large numbers is Dow's sole purpose in life; Welty's evangelist has in fact turned his mission into an obsession. The sunset through which he hurries is simply a part of impenetrable nature, inert unless it can be seen as a sign of the will and mind of the Almighty. It is Dow's abstraction from the world around him that causes him not to notice another rider matching him stride for stride. The second rider is Murrell. The historical Murrell was an outcast and exile from Tennessee, where he had been branded on the thumb for the crime of horse stealing. This was not his only offense. Mayhem, murder, and clannish feuds followed Murrell and his retinue of kin and lowlifes. He found his way to the Natchez region in the early 1830s, as the news and rumors of Nat Turner's insurrection in Virginia was filtering into the area. Murrell used the latent hysteria surrounding the Turner uprising to fuel his own scheme for a slave uprising. Whether Murrell actually intended to lead slaves to freedom, or to use white fear that he would do so to enhance his criminal effectiveness, is a matter of historical debate. Welty uses Murrell's absorption in his plan as the counterpart to Dow's abstraction from the world in the idea of salvation.

The appearance of Audubon breaks the hold of abstraction. Dow and Murrell see the painter but do not know who he is or what errand brings him to this spot. Whether Audubon sees the other two is tantalizingly ambiguous; so rapt is he in pursuit of his art (he has not spoken for days) that he creates a kind of zone around himself that the good or evil of the other two cannot penetrate. True to form, Dow's musings run to theology when he sees the artist, and Murrell's click on his grand scheme for the liberation of the slaves with himself as their messiah.

At the moment these minds intersect, "a solitary snowy heron flew down not far away and began to feed beside the marsh water" (86). Dow sees the bird as an emissary from God, "His love [made] visible" (86). Murrell, shading his eyes against the sunset, sees only the brand of "H.T." (horse thief) on his thumb. Only the artist sees the heron: "Audubon's eyes embraced the object in the distance and he could see it as carefully as if he held it in his hand" (87). Just as carefully, Audubon shoots the heron, for "it was not from that memory that he could paint" (90).

The artist's appropriation of the moment and his breaking of the moment's stillness fracture the group. Dow and Murrell are thrown back upon the assumptions they have brought to nature, not nature itself. Dow's sudden discovery of his separation from the God in nature sparked some of Welty's most moving and revealing writing, a passage Robert Penn Warren, in "The Love and Separateness in Miss Welty,"[7] chose to quote in an early and very influential appraisal of her work:

> The hair rose on his [Dow's] head and his hands began to shake with cold, and suddenly it seemed to him that God Himself, just now, thought of the Idea of Separateness. For surely He had never thought of it before, when the little white heron was flying down to feed. He could understand God's giving Separateness first and then giving Love to follow and heal in its wonder; but God had reversed this, and given Love first and then Separateness, as though it did not matter to Him which came first. (92–93)

Dow is driven to the brink of blasphemy and despair by the fear that God's "plan" in creation might be perverse. He flings himself away from the site of his temptation, automatically curses Satan, and rushes on to his evangelical work.

Reserving the last moment of the story for the man of faith, Welty suggests a balance between art as the empirical knowledge of the things in the world and the craft to represent them, and investment in something unseen that is to come after this world. Murrell, a man of no abstraction but ego, is dismissed first. By undercutting Dow's abstract sense of the word, Welty gives the story itself, the made thing Welty-through-Audubon strove to fashion, the heavier presence. Dow's revelation of the irony of God inventing Love first and then Separateness propels him away from the world rather than into more reverent attention to it. He rushes away to preach on the text "[i]n that day when all hearts shall be disclosed" (94). I Corinthians 4:5, upon which his sermon is based, is an admonition to believers *not* to judge the meaning of human hearts until God has come to do so. Welty's Dow is on his way to do just that.

"First Love" and "A Still Moment" represent the extent to which Welty's creative imagination was drawn to, but hovered above, the historical record accumulated by the Natchez Trace. Balancing history and imagination, she had clearly favored the latter. This is clear in three stories, "Asphodel," "The Wide Net," and "Livvie," that use the Trace primarily as a geography of myth and imagination, a place where indwelling forces of life, rather than historical persons, can take tangible shape in a narrative world. Discussing two of these stories—"Asphodel" for its use of literary imagery and "The Wide Net" for its blending of folk material with *The Divine Comedy*—should give the reader of Welty a sense of her range.

"Asphodel" is the more static of the two stories. Using the actual ruins of Windsor, an opulent house built in 1861 and destroyed by fire in 1890, Welty plays with the static imagery of Keats's "Ode on a Grecian Urn." Three older women, echoing the triad of three ladies who manage Lily Daw, pilgrimage along the Trace to the ruins of Asphodel (Windsor), where they plan a picnic and a ritual recitation of the life and death of Miss Sabina, recently deceased. Miss Sabina had been the wife of the owner of Asphodel, one Don McInnis. The marriage had not been for love; rather, Sabina's father had decreed it and McInnis had treated his wife like a conquered province.

The three McInnis children die. The daughter drowns, a son is killed "in a fall off the wild horse he was bound to ride" (100–101), and a second son shoots himself on the courthouse steps "drunk in the broad daylight" (101). The dynastic ambitions of Don McInnis having been summarily canceled, he takes a mistress into the house. Sabina will not brook such an insult, especially after a record of previous sexual insults, and puts a torch to Asphodel.

Miss Sabina herself is less a character in a realistic narrative of abuse and insult than a static counter in the Keatsian allegory of Apollonian and Dionysian opposites:

> "She [Miss Sabina] was painted to be beautiful and terrible in the face, all dark around the eyes," said Phoebe, "in the way of grand ladies of the South grown old. She wore a fine jet-black wig of great size, for she had lost her hair by some illness or violence. She went draped in the heavy brocades from her family trunks, which she hung about herself in some bitter disregard. She would do no more than pin them and tie them into place. Through such a weight of material her knees pushed slowly, her progress was hampered but she came on. Her look was the challenging one when looks met, though only Miss Sabina knew why there had to be any clangor of encounter among peaceable people. Her hands were small, and as hot to the touch as a child's under the sharp diamonds. One hand, the right one, curved round and clenched an ebony stick mounted with the gold head of a lion." (104–5)

Cora, Irene, and Phoebe tell the eternal story of the clash of gendered opposites with ceremonial formality. Just as they reach the denouement, their antithesis materializes:

> Out into the radiant light with one foot forward had stepped a bearded man. He stood motionless as one of the

columns, his eyes bearing without a break upon the three women. He was as rude and golden as a lion. He did nothing, and he said nothing while the birds sang on. But he was naked. (109)

The old maids flee to their carriage, abandoning the remnants of their picnic and staving off the onslaught of a flock of goats by tossing the one picnic basket held in reserve. That the bearded naked man is symbolic in the same drama as Miss Sabina is confirmed by Cora: "'He was as naked as an old goat. He must be as old as the hills'" (110). That the eternal loggerheads of the entrenched feminine and the equally disruptive masculine still has force is seen fleetingly at the end of "Asphodel" as one of the old maids, Phoebe, laughs aloud as they flee the goats: "she seemed to be still in a tender dream and an unconscious celebration" (113).

"Asphodel" is a tour de force. Welty manipulates the familiar elements of literary discourse with fluid confidence. Keats's urn, symbol of the well-made, integral work as object, is invoked by way of the story's setting on the Natchez Trace. Sabina's father's house and the McInnis house, Asphodel, are situated on a switchback section of the Trace such that they are intimately connected: "almost back to back on the ring of hills, while completely hidden from each other, like the reliefs on opposite sides of a vase" (98). Characters are similarly allegorical; the meanings of each clearly rooted in psychological stereotype. If "Asphodel" has a flaw it may in fact be its virtuosity, for once the reader gets the fit of two pieces, the whole falls into place with a kind of inevitable efficiency.

"The Wide Net" has much in common with "Asphodel." Both stories stereotype the genders and place them at an eternal barricade of opposition. Character is determined not by realistic demands of time and place but rather by the needs of the allegory of male and female. Literary allusions are tangible, yet not as obvious as those in "Asphodel." The Trace is used as the locale of imaginative free-play, not historical discipline to event and date. Whereas the subtext of "Asphodel" is replete with borrowings from classical mythology, the high canon of English literature, the subtext of "The Wide Net," with a few exceptions, is redolent of tall tale and folklore.

William Wallace Jamieson, ironically named for the Braveheart of Highland legend, and his wife, Hazel, are expecting their first child, and the confirmation of his potency seems to have suggested to William Wallace that a hell-raising session with some of his pals is in order. Straggling home the next morning with his aptly named sidekick, Virgil, William Wallace finds no Hazel to welcome him. Instead, he finds a note informing him that she has drowned herself in the Pearl River. William Wallace then conscripts Virgil and most of the male population of Dover into his quest to drag the river for Hazel's body. For this he will need the wide net and Doc, its owner.

At this point, preliminaries of narrative established, the plot of "The Wide Net" settles into a comfortable tall-tale mode. William Wallace reminisces about his courting of Hazel, Hazel's mother's resistance, his vanquishing of the battle-ax's opposition. Virgil comments in a melancholy aside that it is a pity that women get old and become just like their mothers (38). Like the Pied Piper of Hamelin, William Wallace collects

Doyles and Malones and two Negro boys without last names.
Doc decides to accompany his net; on the way to the Pearl he
dispenses a kind of cracker-barrel commentary:

> "We're walking along in the changing-time," said Doc.
> "Any day now the change will come. It's going to turn
> from hot to cold, and we can kill the hog that's ripe and
> have fresh meat to eat." (48)

Solstices and equinoxes Welty uses with regularity and modu-
lated degrees of self-consciousness and seriousness. Doc's
utterance indicates that the time is unstable, liminal, and that
the river party can expect just about anything *except* the ordinary.

The party drags the river for most of the afternoon, recovering a load of junk and plenty of fish, but no Hazel. Forgetting
for the moment their sad errand, they decide to have a big fish
fry. The meal quickly becomes a tribal ceremony. Sensing
rather than actually knowing the group to be seated in a ring,
William Wallace jumps into the center and is transported into a
kind of buck dance:

> But William Wallace answered none of them anything,
> for he was leaping all over the place and all over them
> and the feast and the bones of the feast, trampling the
> sand, up and down, and doing a dance so crazy that he
> would die next. He took a big catfish and hooked it to his
> belt buckle and went up and down so that they all
> hollered, and the tears of laughter streaming down his

cheeks made him put his hand up, and the two days' growth of beard began to jump out, bright red. (59)

William Wallace's priapic celebration seems to summon from the mystical conditions of the place a kindred spirit. Out of the Pearl River comes a creature of "a long dark body" and hoary head that all present recognize at once as the "King of Snakes" (60). The monster and William Wallace stare at each other for a few moments, then the King of Snakes returns to his lair in the Pearl. The suspense of the moment is broken by a storm, punctuating the change of seasons, which barrels through the area and puts an end to the ceremony of the river. The party must return to the town of Dover, an exhausted and used-up place. The entry of the triumphant men and boys with their load of fish and boasting stories lights up Dover. But William Wallace has still not found Hazel.

As the sun sets, William Wallace and Virgil climb a hill and, looking down on Dover, they hear the tunes of the Sacred Harp Sing traveling on the still wind. The moment makes William Wallace aware of something like the need for complementarity in human life: his rough, priapic stomping *and* the delicate (female) notes of the Sacred Harp:

They were having the Sacred Harp Sing on the grounds of an old white church glimmering there at the crossroads, far below. He stared away as if he saw it minutely, as if he could see a lady in white take a flowered cover off the organ, which was set on a little slant in the shade, dust the keys, and start to pump and play. . . . He smiled

faintly, as he would at his mother, and at Hazel, and at the
singing women in his life, now all one young girl standing up to sing under the tree the oldest and longest bal-
lads there were. (70)

Crossroads are junctions of difference; in "The Wide Net," as in
a good many of Welty's works, the difference is gendered.
William Wallace's hilltop vision, allusive of such vistas afforded
Virgil and his charge in *The Divine Comedy,* puts before him the
truth he did not know he was seeking in the Pearl River. Having
achieved the knowledge, if not the self-knowledge, of the need
for complementaries, William Wallace may now reunite with his
Beatrice.

Hazel had never had any intention of drowning herself. She
had been hiding in the house the whole time, close enough to
touch William Wallace when he read her note. Her point made,
the two slip comfortably into former habits: William Wallace
spanks Hazel, and she protests. But the last "word" is hers. She
will do the same thing again if she chooses, she tells her husband.
Then Hazel tells him when it is time to go into the house, to bed:

He climbed to his feet too and stood beside her, with the
frown on his face, trying to look where she looked. And
after a few minutes she took him by the hand and led him
into the house, smiling as if she were smiling down on
him. (72)

Welty has given Hazel the all-powerful smile, the all-knowing
look. The divisions between male and female, couched in folk-

loric terms in "The Wide Net," are smoothed over. The procreative couple who retreat to their intimacy at the end of the story have found a way to make their differences complementary. Hazel and William Wallace have what R. J. Bowman saw with his life's last glances in "Death of a Traveling Salesman": a fruitful marriage. "The Wide Net," dedicated to her friend John Fraiser Robinson, is one of the happiest stories Eudora Welty wrote.

Three of the last four stories of *The Wide Net,* however, are not so happy. Separations and estrangements that seem so happily overcome in other stories remain unhealed in "The Purple Hat," "The Winds," and "At the Landing." The Natchez Trace, when it is named in the stories, becomes a type of the downward and inward spiral into regions of the unconscious usually held at bay.

"The Purple Hat" takes place in a French Quarter bar in New Orleans, far from the actual Natchez Trace. Neither the narrator nor any character in the story mentions the Trace. Welty was, in fact, unsure that "The Purple Hat" belonged in *The Wide Net,* but Russell assured her its presence would not detract from the quality of the ensemble. "The Purple Hat" plainly introduces readers of *The Wide Net* to the downward spiral of association that leads to the unconscious level where literary tidiness is not always possible. These three stories center primarily on sex and the anxiety of initiation. The repertoire of symbol and allusion is more frankly Freudian or psychoanalytic, less literary and cultural.

"The Purple Hat" is a brief story, the shortest in *The Wide Net.* Three men are in a dim bar in the French Quarter on a rainy afternoon. One is the bartender, the second is an employee of a casino whose job is to watch the tables from concealed vantage points, the third is a young man drinking desperately and clearly the worse for some unexpressed tension. The second man tells the story of an older woman in a purple hat who gambles at his casino with a succession of younger men, whose money she drains without repaying in sexual or other favors. He has seen her murdered twice in the span of thirty years (146).

The tradition of the gothic ghost story is replete with "demon lover" tales, and Welty scarcely strays from the formula. The young man at the bar is the old ghost's most recent human lover—perhaps her most recent murderer too. Is it the act of murder or the act of love that agitates the young man?

The purple hat pushes Welty's use of symbolism in sexual directions the two following stories require. At a certain moment of the evening at the gaming tables, the old woman removes the purple hat:

> He [the young man] is enamored of her hat—her ancient, battered, outrageous hat with the awful plush flowers. She lays it down below the level of the table there, on her shabby old lap, and he caresses it. . . . Well, I suppose in this town there are stranger forms of love than that, and who are any of us to say what ways people may not find to love? She herself, you know, seems perfectly satisfied with it. And yet she must not be satisfied, being a ghost. (149)

"The awful plush flowers," so magnified in Welty's imagery when moved to the secreted space of the woman's lap where the young man "caresses" them, demarcate the clear zone of sexual symbolism.

How should this symbolism be read in "The Purple Hat"? In one way, as self-conscious farce; the hat spoofs the sexual tension that is one of the necessary undercurrents of the gothic ghost story. Another way of reading the sexual theme and symbolism is to confine it just to Welty's own work, and within that body of work to the stories in *The Wide Net*. Although not all of the stories place sexuality centrally as theme, several do. And much of the work Welty was to do after *The Wide Net* has been explored by critics as deeply devoted to investigating the intricacies of sex and gender and the systems of representation our culture continues to develop for discussing such powerful topics.

"The Winds" is an eloquent case in point. When Welty initially sent the manuscript of the story to her agent, he recognized it as a difficult sell—that is, difficult to sell to any magazine that did not specialize in a female readership. Sensing that "The Winds" was a "girls' story," Russell decided to let it be purchased by *Harper's Bazaar,* a leading women's fashion magazine.[8] The literary editor who bought "The Winds," Mary Lou Aswell, and Welty began a correspondence that became a life-long friendship.

Russell's intuition about "The Winds" and his relegation of it to a woman's magazine and a female readership constitute a form of self-defense. Traditional images of male sexuality, as in the figure of Don McInnis in "Asphodel," are not often flattering in Welty's stories. Especially is this so in "The Winds" and the story that followed it, "At the Landing."

"The Winds" opens with the approach of a summer equinoctial storm upon the house where Josie, the central character, her younger brother Will, and her parents live in four-square harmony and stability. Josie, twelve years old and dreaming a little about what "big girls" might know about and do with boys, is awakened by her father as the storm approaches; he wants the family to move to a more secure part of the house. Josie thinks the commotion might come from a picnic or hayride out on Natchez Trace—here also known as Lover's Lane—but her father explains in simple declarative sentences that "this is the equinox" and that such a change in weather occurs twice a year, summer and winter (117). The meteorological explanation, however, is useless to Josie.

Josie's mother might know a more significant answer to her daughter's curiosity, but she is cryptic in her statements. "Unlike herself," Josie's mother aggressively chooses to hold Josie in the storm (117). Thus the lines of gender and sex are marked. The lines are deepened when Josie looks for a neighbor girl, Cornella, out in the storm. Josie's mother is adamant that "'you need not concern yourself with—Cornella!' The way her mother said her name was not diminished now" (118). Josie has been sparked to some degree of curiosity about the blonde older girl, and the potential alienation of her identification with the outsider bothers her mother.

Something deeper also disturbs the mother, though, and prompts her to utter mysterious things. As the house shakes in the strong winds, Josie's mother sighs, "'Summer is over'" (119). Josie's mother's words have meaning beyond the actual seasons; the mother understands "summer" as a code word for another condition—Josie's childhood, for example. This reading seems confirmed when, a few lines later in the story, the narrator discloses that the persistent lightning "seemed slowly to be waking something that slept longer than Josie had slept" under her mother's watchfulness (119). "'Be still,' said her mother. 'It's soon over'" (120). "It," Josie's maturation and the development of her acceptance of it, is just beginning.

This maturation and acceptance progresses through flashbacks that evoke the image of Cornella and her powerful place in Josie's reverie. In her imaginative life Josie searches for a female archetype; she conducts private rituals in the forest during which she calls for female immersion: "'I am thine eternally, my Queen, and will serve thee always and I will be enchanted with thy love forever'" (121). That this intuitive thirst for female identification might also be sexual is implied by the way Josie rides her bicycle, named "the golden Princess":

> She would take her [the bicycle] as early as possible. So as to touch nothing, to make no print on the earliness of the day, she rode with no hands, no feet, touching nowhere but the one place, moving away into the leaves, down the swaying black boards of the dewy alley. (121)

The sexual meanings wrought into the bicycle and her stimulating way of riding migrate smoothly into memories of Cornella, a second "golden Princess" by virtue of her flowing blonde hair and her symbolic "captivity" in a household of cousins. Josie succumbs to desire for Cornella; she wants to love the older girl. Cornella, however, aware of Josie's attention repeatedly stamps her foot as if to terminate the spell (124, 125).

The house survives the storm, and the next day the family goes together to a Chautauqua. Here, Josie and Cornella meet again as both are mesmerized by a female cornetist. This woman might be the archetype Josie has sought:

> There in the flame-like glare that was somehow shadowy, she had come from far away, and the long times of the world seemed to be about her. She was draped heavily in white, shaded with blue, like a Queen, and she stood braced and looking upward like the figure-head on a Viking ship. As the song drew out, Josie could see the slow appearance of a little vein in her cheek. Her closed eyelids seemed almost to whir and yet to rest motionless, like the wings of a humming-bird, when she reached the high note. (137)

Cornella is also in the audience, likewise mesmerized by the Valkyrie's ecstasy. Triangulated in desire, Josie and Cornella become superimposed personae. Next morning, Josie finds a note clearly intended for Cornella but finding its way to Josie: "'O my darling I have waited so long when are you coming for me? Never a day or a night goes by that I do not ask When? When? When?'" (140). Although Josie has literally *not* written the note, she appropriates it to her consciousness as if she had, for she hides it in "her most secret place, the little drawstring bag that held her dancing shoes" (140).

Clearly, Russell was right: "The Winds" is a girl's story. Josie, one of the most autobiographical characters Welty had yet constructed, is the armature of a more elaborate construction of female change, maturation, negotiation with experience that is clearly sexual but still hazy as to what form that sexuality will take.[9] As in previous stories, the figures of masculinity in "The Winds," Josie's father and her brother Will, are clearly bracketed apart from the central action. Josie's reverie and her triangulated passion for Cornella underline that theme. If the conclusion of the story is unstable, that is appropriate; Josie has reached a threshold but has not moved beyond it.

"At the Landing" is the darkest story in *The Wide Net,* the last one written for the collection (completed in the latter half of 1942), the one that left Russell with the deepest sense of incompletion, and the one that left the author with a strong sense of being wrung out by the Natchez process. In a sense, Jenny in "At the Landing" extends Josie's "ride" into experience. Harriet Pollack explores this avenue of meaning and links "At the Landing" through *The Robber Bridegroom* to Welty's "private" system of allusion.[10] Welty, who professed to her agent that "At the Landing" took her places she could not anticipate, nevertheless pressed her experiments in symbolic expression of the unconscious beyond any boundary she had yet confronted.[11]

Sharing with "The Winds" the usage of night and storm as the symbolic envelope of unconscious meaning, "At the Landing" opens with the image of night and the dream of high water. The night of his death, Jenny's grandfather comes to her bedroom door with his nightmare of flood foretold by the figure of Floyd, a river man who is identified by the sinister side of appetites in William Wallace: Floyd sports a "great long catfish" on his wrist like a talisman (178). Floyd's phallic sign metamorphoses, from the point of view of Jenny, into the "cord and tassel" of her grandfather's robe (179). The room Jenny sleeps in had been her mother's; it had been barred on the outside when her mother slept there. Male sexual aggression and female immurement: the geography of Jenny's condition is hostile.

Escape is the clear goal. Jenny, however, motherless and, until the death of her grandfather, obliged to care for the old man, has little imagination for or of the outside world into which she might flee, and less nerve for the ordeal. Her mother had died in captivity yearning for a taste of the outside as limited as Natchez. That kind of imaginative and emotional starvation has carried over into the daughter.

After the death of her grandfather, the figure of Floyd with his emblem, the great long fish, walks through Jenny's imagination as he actually strolls through the landing. Floyd is an archetypal figure: relentlessly male, unconfined by responsibilities or mores, free by self-declaration from pausing between the moment of appetite and taking what fills it. He is the antithesis to Jenny, and of course they mark each other on collision course:

> But she knew what she would find when she would come to him. She would find him equally real with herself—and could not touch him then. As she was living and inviolate, so of course was he, and when that gave him delight, how could she bring a question to him? She walked in the woods and around the graves in it, and knew about love, how it would have a different story in the world if it could lose the moral knowledge of a mys-

> tery that is in the other heart. Nothing in Floyd frightened
> her that drew her near, but at once she had the knowledge
> come to her that fragile mystery was in everyone and in
> herself, since there it was in Floyd, and that whatever she
> did, she would be bound to ride over and hurt, and the
> secrecy of life was the terror of it. When Floyd rode the
> red horse, she lay in the grass. He might even have
> jumped across her. But the vaunting and prostration of
> love told her nothing—nothing at all. (188–89)

Jenny's thinly veiled dream of sexual intercourse, and the
physical as well as emotional loss in store for her in the act,
serve as foreshadowed denouement of "At the Landing."
Events of plot and symbolism all point toward that end.

As the flood came with Floyd as its prophet in the grandfather's dream, an actual flood comes with Floyd as its human
manifestation and sweeps Jenny along. Stranded on high
ground, Jenny and Floyd act out a kind of savage pastoral.
Floyd violates Jenny without a sign of the act's moral impact
on him, then feeds her fish he has cooked himself until she
vomits the excess (200–201). Just as obliviously, Floyd aban-
dons Jenny when the waters recede.

Floyd has left a mark on Jenny, and the people of the landing can see it as clearly as if it were a birthmark or tattoo. At
first, Jenny believes that she feels love and that Floyd loves her
in return, even though he is nowhere to be seen. Whenever she
remembers their solitary moments, Jenny trembles and is convinced that the trembling is the reality of love. Time, though,
cures her of that misapprehension:

> But at last the trembling left and dull strength came back, as if a wound had ceased to flow its blood. And then one day in summer she could look at a bird flying in the air, its tiny body like a fist opening and closing, and did not feel daze or pain, and then she was healed of the shock of love. (205)

In the void left by the departure of any meaning beyond the literal identification of the thing, "despair" enters Jenny's life and fills it (212).

Paradoxically, despair empowers her to leave the landing. She wanders off in search of Floyd, ending up on the river among a community of gypsy fishermen. Jenny waits most of the day for Floyd to appear. The women cook and clean nets while the men menacingly toss knives at a tree. At full dark the inevitable occurs: the men put Jenny in a grounded houseboat and one by one rape her. The trauma turns out to be beneficial, for the formerly introverted Jenny "now . . . could speak to everyone, in a vague stir of welcome or in the humility that moved now deep in her spirit" (213). Her chrysalis of innocence shattered, Jenny enters a community of human beings in the world. Her entry, following the motif of the return of Persephone in "Livvie" and many other stories by Welty, is known by the women and children of the fishing community who do not actually witness Jenny's violation, but know it as if they had:

> A rude laugh covered her cry, and somehow both the harsh human sounds could easily have been heard as rejoicing, going out over the river in the dark night. By

the fire, little boys were slapped crossly by their mothers—as if they knew that the original smile now crossed
Jenny's face, and hung there no matter what was done to
her, like a bit of color that kindles in the sky after the
light has gone. (214)

By some contemporary standards of sexual politics, the ending
to "At the Landing" condones rape. It was inevitable that Jenny
enter experience; the actual circumstances are irrelevant. Such a
reading of the story might err on the side of literalness; what happens to Jenny is not a literal rape, but rather a representation of
the forcible appropriation of her, body and spirit, to a truly
human community that surpasses in *potential* value the repres-
sive one from which she has been released by the death of the
patriarch, her grandfather. For the author to select the act of rape
to represent Jenny's reinitiation could be read as her intention to
emphasize the importance of that passage for Jenny.

There is more to be said for the latter interpretation. Jenny
is not the only vulnerable female protagonist in Welty's early
fiction to face or to complete such a passage. Rosamond Musgrove, the heroine of *The Robber Bridegroom,* seems to romp
unscathed from rape to social comfort. Pollack, exploring the
continuity of the story and novella, finds a darker tinge to Rosamond that relates her more intimately to Jenny Lockhart.[12]
Ruby Fisher, in "A Piece of News," seems to thrive on sexual
liaisons with strange men; in a different register, the women of
"Petrified Man" seem energized by the threat and news of rape.
In *The Wide Net,* the motif of sexual initiation/violation operates in several stories in several ways. In the title story, clearly,

Hazel could not occupy the elevated and elevating position of Madonna were she not pregnant. Livvie's marriage to Solomon is almost certainly chaste; she is untouched and isolated from the world until Cash takes her away. The ghost woman in "The Purple Hat" is reduced, by the power of the symbolism of her hat, to her sexuality. Josie's passage, in "The Winds," takes her to the threshold of sexual knowledge, then leaves her and the story poised at the next step. "At the Landing" is, by virtue of its placement in *The Wide Net,* the next step in the journey of a progressively developing female protagonist. Indeed, one way to read development into the work of the first decade of Welty's career as a published writer is to trace the emergence of this composite "character" as she gradually appears amid an array of literary experiments with voice and point of view, style, subject matter, and narrative structure. Most of what Welty had learned from the trying-out period of her career she began to consolidate in her first novel, *Delta Wedding.*

CHAPTER FOUR

Delta Wedding

Delta Wedding, serialized in four installments in *Atlantic Monthly* from January through April 1946, is Welty's first novel. Like many published novels, it appears perfectly finished, ready for reading and interpretation. But ever since her first unsuccessful encounters with publishers, who politely insisted on a novel before they would consider a book of her short stories, Welty had decided to invest her talent in the short story. She had concluded that the novel obligated an author to obey the standards of historical realism—accounting for the who, what, when, where, and why of things—a direction she could not see for her work.

Welty had, in fact, tried the novel at least once. Little survives of the "novel" she submitted, partially in outline, to the Houghton Mifflin first-novel contest in 1938. Robert Penn Warren and Cleanth Brooks, editors of the *Southern Review,* had recommended Welty for the Houghton Mifflin prize. Katherine Anne Porter was also a sponsor. Even though Welty's submission rated an "A," it did not take the publication prize.

After such early setbacks, Welty decided to model her writing career on Porter's, dedicating herself to the craft and tradition of the short story. She worked closely with Porter at Yaddo in 1941, watching the senior writer struggle with "No Safe Harbor," the novel that was not to be finished until 1962, when it appeared as *Ship of Fools.* Welty did not want to get into a twenty-year project that might or might not bear fruit.

But a few years later her novel was happening anyway. In an interview with Charles T. Bunting in 1972, Welty remembered some of the circumstances surrounding *Delta Wedding:*

> I'm sorry; I can't even remember planning *Delta Wedding.* But one piece of work doesn't affect another, at any rate. *Delta Wedding* did begin as a short story. It was Diarmuid Russell who told me it was a novel. I sent in something called "The Delta Cousins," and he read it and sent it back and said, "This is Chapter Two of a novel," which it is. (*Conversations* 47)

Even earlier, Russell had commented that certain short stories seemed unfinished and truncated: "The Winds" and "At the Landing," for example. Welty's vision was beginning to demand a range longer and wider than the short story usually provided, and her craft was stretched to keep up.

Although Welty had read many novels and practiced many kinds of narrative writing, writing the novel by any traditional mode of constructing character and narrative was an unpleasant option. Following realistic narrative guidelines was not among Welty's ambitions, but she needed a trailblazer to show her how the novel, so closely identified with such narrative conventions as cause and effect and such character traditions as plausible psychology, might otherwise be written. In the process of revising "The Delta Cousins" into the novel that she tentatively agreed that it was, Welty found, in Virginia Woolf, the trailblazer she sought.

Welty reviewed Woolf's posthumous *A Haunted House and Other Stories* in the *New York Times Book Review* on April 16,

1944. One of the pieces in Woolf's collection, "An Unwritten Novel," showed Welty how to complete her own struggling novel. The crucial insight is both technical and psychological: point of view—contrary to the realistic rule—need not be unified in one central consciousness, and the membrane between one human consciousness and another is not a thick rind but permeable tissue:

> In the experience of observing, the observer is herself observed, her deft plunges into another's obscure background become reachings into her own hidden future, error makes and cancels error, until identification between the characters examined and the writer examining seems fluid, electric, passing back and forth. (*New York Times Book Review* 3)

Fluid, electric, permeable—but not judgmental. The centralized and unified point of view of the realistic novel polices a work, asserting the status quo. Welty, never using such political language, sought a way to thwart control without sacrificing all form. She found her example in Woolf, whose feminist vision, as interpreted by Carolyn G. Heilbrun in *Hamlet's Mother* (1990), runs uncannily true to Welty's temperament.

Welty fragments realistic point of view—one of Woolf's fundamental innovations to the realistic status quo. Whereas a traditional novel will have a unified and consistent point of view or narrating voice, Welty chose to use several, all female, in *Delta Wedding*. The omniscient point of view in the novel spends less time actually telling the story than orchestrating the telling by several female presences: Laura McRaven, the nine-year-old Fairchild cousin who is invited to Dabney Fairchild's wedding; Ellen Fairchild, the mother of the sprawling Delta family; Dabney, the marrying daughter; Shelley, the oldest daughter worried a little about *not* wanting to get married; Robbie Reid, estranged wife of George Fairchild. Other voices contribute briefer sections of the action.

Since the narrating center is kaleidoscopically divided up, the action does not run on a central line, by simple cause and effect, from one historical event to the next. It is true that the action of *Delta Wedding* takes place on a closely paced calendar: the week leading up to Dabney's Saturday wedding, and then a picnic three days later. But the meaningful action of the novel is far from dependent on this cause-and-effect chronology. That the majority of reviewers of the novel in 1946 complained, with varying degrees of discomfort, that "nothing happens" in *Delta Wedding* reinforces its nontraditional technique. As a novelist, Welty was out in front of her readers.

Early in the novel we are given a strong hint that chronological time will probably be dismissed: "Then Aunt Ellen came in, meditatively, as the hall clock finished striking two which meant it was eight" (20). Faulkner, who seems to have his fingerprints on every device any other southern writer ever tried, used the same misstriking clock in *The Sound and the Fury* to tell something about Dilsey's mythic character. Welty uses it to decree freedom from the realism that time dictates. Her plot, rather, moves by a rhythm of repetition and variation, circling back upon itself before moving forward.

Late in *Delta Wedding,* riding to the twilight picnic which ends the wedding celebration, Ellen Fairchild, the central (female) consciousness, reflects on the novel's events. She muses, though, *not* on the meaning of what has happened but on the pattern that human experience takes:

> Ellen at Battle's [her husband's] side rode looking ahead, they were comfortable and silent, both, with their great weight, breathing a little heavily in a rhythm that brought them sometimes together. The repeating fields, the repeating cycles of season and her own life—there was something in the monotony itself that was beautiful, rewarding—perhaps to what was womanly within her. (240)

The invocation of rhythm and repetition as the structural principle of *Delta Wedding* distinguishes it from the traditional realistic novel.

Circling and repetition, since they bring the reader back over territory that seems to have been covered already, create the effect of slowing time, delaying outcomes, preventing the entropy that erodes whatever human happiness might be won. Because of this effect, structure overtakes meaning in *Delta Wedding.* As Hamilton Basso put it in his review, "Although nothing 'happens' in *Delta Wedding . . . everything* happens."[1] Dabney's aunts fret about her "leaving the Delta" because of her marriage, thereby permitting a hint of entropy or decay to infiltrate the tight Fairchild circle. Ellen, Dabney's mother, worries about the risk her daughter faces in her marriage to Troy Flavin; Ellen cannot but know Dabney as both child and woman, at once immune to destructive change and rushing headlong into it. Shelley, the oldest daughter and the one most skeptical of life, writes in her diary that Fairchilds "never wanted to be smart, one by one, but all together we have a wall, we are self-sufficient against people that come up knocking, we are solid to the outside" (84). Aunt Shannon, old and deaf, confuses younger members of the family with the dead, thus reinforcing the theme of stopped or slowed time within the inviolate circle of Shellmound.

Sharpening her own technical practice in the short story, Welty had learned the central modernist lesson that form is meaning. Reading Woolf crystallized the lesson. To adapt her short-story technique to the rigors of the novel was not easy, but she had a guide. Growth required careful thinking even from the stage of preliminaries. Welty had to find a year, a historical date, that could seem to function as the objective correlative of "the real," but would do so without obliging her to narrate events:

> I chose those [decades of 1920s for *Delta Wedding,* 1930s for *Losing Battles*] for very particular reasons. In the case of *Delta Wedding* I chose the twenties—when I was more the age of my little girl [Laura in the novel], which was why I thought best to have a child in it. But in writing about the Delta, I had to pick a year—and this was quite hard to do— in which all the men could be home and uninvolved. It couldn't be a war year. It couldn't be a year when there was a flood in the Delta because those were the times before the flood control. It had to be a year that would leave my characters all free to have a family story. It meant looking in the almanac—in fact, I did—to find a year that was uneventful

and that would allow me to concentrate on the people without any undue outside influences; I wanted to write a story that showed the solidity of this family and the life that went on on a small scale in a world of its own. (*Conversations* 49–50)

Realism in the novel, as Welty implies, is quasi-political; once an author gives in to history (war, flood), she gives up imaginative control, for there is always the who, what, and why of the public record to be appeased. Whatever happens in history makes whatever happens elsewhere subordinate, not important. Welty moved peremptorily, in writing *Delta Wedding,* not to eliminate history entirely but to destabilize it, thus marginalizing the males for whom history is the arena of meaning and power, and opening room for the women who are traditionally shut out of public action.

To substitute for the structural stability history can provide, Welty supplied internal stability in repetition. In the dynasty of the Fairchilds of Shellmound, names of the sons recur over the generations: George, Denis, Battle. The child in Ellen's womb will carry the name Denis—if he is a boy. Ellen's pregnancy is her tenth, adding natural repetition to the manmade repetition of naming. Dabney's marriage to the overseer Troy, a man from the hills of northeastern Mississippi, repeats the marriage of George to Robbie Reid, an outsider in terms of class—her father was a storekeeper.

By far the most important element in the pattern of structural repetition is the inset narrative of the Yellow Dog episode: the incident in which the Yazoo Delta locomotive (the Yellow Dog) nearly annihilated the Fairchild clan. Told or alluded to at least ten times in *Delta Wedding,* the Yellow Dog episode functions as the author's self-conscious declaration of the coupling of theme—"the solidity of this family and the life that went on on a small scale in a world of its own"—and narrative technique, for the Yellow Dog episode is narrated in a range of literary styles that, taken together, testify to Welty's self-conscious plan to negate realistic, progressive narrative.

The first to narrate is Orrin Fairchild, the oldest son. His style is the most straightforward and "novelistic," serving as a norm against which to play variations. Orrin, his finger holding his place in a book, tells Laura "the way it was":

> The whole family but Papa and Mama, and ten or twenty Negroes with us, went fishing in Drowning Lake. It will be two weeks ago Sunday. And so coming home we walked the track. We were tired—we were singing. On the trestle Maureen danced and caught her foot. I've done that, but I know how to get loose. [Maureen, nine years old, is brain damaged.] Uncle George kneeled down and went to work on Maureen's foot, and the train came. He hadn't got Maureen's foot loose, so he didn't jump either. The rest of us did jump, and the Dog stopped just before it hit them and ground them all to pieces. (19)

The requisite elements of narrative are present: who, what, when, where, how. The climax is rushed and underplayed, reflecting both Orrin's matter-of-fact character and the thin satisfactions of historical narrative as Welty would rate them.

India Fairchild, at nine years old Laura's counterpart *inside* the family, is the next to tell the story. India embroiders where her brother had merely stitched for function. "'I can tell it good—make everybody cry,'" India claims. "'It was late in the afternoon!' cried India, joining her hands . . . 'Just before the thunderstorm'" (58–59). Melodrama is India's forte. She knows how to build suspense into her version; she accelerates the action syntactically: "'And then we didn't catch nothing. Came home on the railroad track, came through the swamp. Came to the trestle'" (59). The story in India's version shoots toward its climax:

> "We started across [the trestle]. Then Shelley couldn't walk it either. She's supposed to be such a tomboy! And she couldn't look down. Everybody knows there isn't any water in Dry Creek in the summertime. . . . Well, Shelley went down the bank and walked through it. I was singing a song I know. 'I'll measure my love to show you, I'll measure my love to show you—.' . . . Then Shelley said, 'Look! Look! The Dog!' and she yelled like a banshee and the Yellow Dog was coming creep-creep down the track with a flag on it. . . . We said, 'Wait, wait! Go back! Stop! Don't run over us!' But *it* didn't care!" (59)

India's narrative is the polar opposite of her brother's. Where Orrin's narrative is spare and factual, India's is evocative, studded with keys to audience response—all extreme, all emotional. India has clearly seen a few of the silent movie melodramas (mentioned by several of the characters in the novel) in which the villain ties the heroine to the railroad tracks as the puffing locomotive bears down. Where her brother's version keeps to the straight and narrow, India's is full of detours, delays. The pleasure is in the telling for India, not in the completion of the story.

Maureen "tells" her own version of the story in starkly minimalist style. Playing hide-and-seek with Laura and her brothers and sisters, Maureen, because of her handicap, is an unknown factor. She might follow the rules of the game, she might not. But it is she who finds Laura hiding behind a pile of logs. Maureen springs to the top of the stack and sends the pile cascading down upon Laura, chanting "choo choo" (74). Maureen narrates remembered experience in a way similar to Benjy in Faulkner's *The Sound and the Fury*.

Shelley, the one member of the family who spends a lot of her time seeking privacy and using it to write the chronicle of the Fairchild life in her diary, has perhaps the most multilayered version of the Yellow Dog episode:

The scene on the trestle was so familiar as to be almost indelible in Shelley's head, for her memory arrested the action and let her see it again and again, like a painting in a schoolroom, with colors vivid and thunderclouded, George and Maureen above locked together, and the others below with the shadow of the trestle on them. The engine with two wings of smoke above it, soft as a big bird, was upon them, coming as it would. George was no longer working at Maureen's caught foot. Their faces fixed, and in the instant alike, Maureen and Uncle George seemed to wait for the blow. Maureen's arms had spread across the path of the engine.

Shelley knew what had happened next, but the greatest
pressure of uneasiness let her go after the one moment, as
if the rest were a feat, a trick that would not work twice.
The engine came to a stop. The tumbling denouement
was what made them all laugh at the table. The apology
of the engineer, old sleepy-head Mr. Doolittle that traded
at the store! Shelley beat her head a time or two on the
wall. And Maureen with no warning pushed with both
her strong hands on George's chest, and he went over
backwards to fall from the trestle, fall down in the vines
to little Ranny's and ole Sylvanus' wild cries. George did
not even yet let her go, his hand reached for her pum-
meling hand and what he could not accomplish by loos-
ening her foot or by pulling her up free, he accomplished
by falling himself. Wrenched bodily, her heavy foot
lifted and Maureen fell with him. And all the time the
Dog had stopped. (87)

Shelley sees too much ever to be happy, for what she sees tells
her that experience is not designed with meaning included.
What should, must, be a readable lesson in heroism and bless-
ings on the Fairchild family, is in fact an absurdist counter-
drama in which the damsel rejects the savior and in so doing
saves both herself and the savior from a fate that has already
ceased to threaten either one. Try as she might to layer the narrative with metaphor, simile, and a sentence pattern of cumulative participles, Shelley cannot change the outcome: human
subjects of experience have no power to control what happens
to them—survive or perish willy-nilly.

Subsequent renarrations of the Yellow Dog episode stitch
the cyclical progress of *Delta Wedding* into a controlled spiral.
Roy Fairchild, Laura's male counterpart, is reported to have
told the story with interpretation supplied by his Aunt Tempe
(115). Robbie Reid, forcefully repatriated into the Fairchild
clan after leaving George and their marriage, tells it disjoint-
edly with herself as the focal point (142, 146, 186). The general
narrative voice of the novel sums it up from the Fairchild collective point of view (188). Ellen, seeing George in the lumi-
nous paper-lantern light of the wedding reception, retells the
Yellow Dog story privately to herself, lighting on the meaning
of George in the story and in the collective life of the Fairchild
clan (221). It is "told" with more serious structural variations in
the report of the death on the tracks of the unnamed young
white girl whom Ellen meets in the woods near Troy's overseer
house (70, 218), and in Shelley's stunt of speeding over the
crossing in front of the Yellow Dog the Sunday after Dabney's
wedding (234). Mr. Doolittle stops in time again.

Welty uses the repetition of the Yellow Dog episode for
structural coherence and thematic unity in place of the linear,
public saga of the wedding. The logical continuation of cause
and effect from plot-event to plot-event is only one way to
achieve the goal of narrative coherence, and it never was the
way Welty preferred to take her writing. Primarily from Virginia Woolf, a mentor whom she repeatedly acknowledged,[2]
Welty learned that a pattern of repetition of event, symbol, or
motif with variation could also achieve narrative coherence.
Indeed, repetition in narrative could achieve a qualitatively *different,* because more concentrated, form of coherence—the

kind of unity compositions in music and in painting often achieve. Both painting and music are art forms in which Welty felt comfortable and empowered. In *Delta Wedding* she uses the Yellow Dog episode as a composer might use a recurrent theme, changing tempo or key with each repetition. By structuring *Delta Wedding* this way, Welty makes a literary-political point. She, like Woolf, positions herself as an insurgent against the control of imagination by history and realism. Probably unintentionally, she got herself embroiled in politics because of her literary stand.

Reviewers of the novel made political assumptions front and center. The most notorious review, assuming that Welty could do no better because of her region and her sex, came from Diana Trilling. Finding Welty's peers to be only women writers (Katherine Mansfield, Sylvia Townsend Warner, Christina Stead, Edita Morris), Trilling then finishes with a condemnation of Welty's region:

For in the best of her stories, and they were the earliest ones, Miss Welty gave us what was really a new view of the South, indeed a new kind of realism about the South; and for this she used, not a dance prose, but a prose that walked on its feet in the world of reality. But increasingly Miss Welty has turned away from the lower-middle-class milieu of, say, The Petrified Man, to that part of the Southern scene which is most available to myth and celebrative legend and, in general, to the narcissistic Southern fantasy; and for this her prose has risen more and more on tiptoe.[3] (Champion 105)

Diana Trilling was not alone in bashing *Delta Wedding* for what she concluded was its defense of the South. Isaac Rosenfeld panned it in the *New Republic,* and New Orleanian Harnett Kane complained that *Delta Wedding* did not contain sufficient politics of the liberal kind.[4]

Readers and literary critics have, by and large, had to catch up with the novel. Appreciations of its formal intricacy understandably awaited the development of American (and southern) formalist criticism: the New Criticism. Schooled in New Critical attention, teachers of literature and critics began to see thematic unity as a direct product of the repetition of the Yellow Dog episode. In each telling of the emergency on the trestle, some aspect of the range of meanings encompassed by personal identity and communal identity is assessed and positioned. Robbie Reid, for example, rails against the assumptions of the Fairchild clan as acted out by their hero, her husband, George Fairchild. In Robbie's view, the automatic assumption of the clan that the one member designated "sometimes almost its hero and sometimes almost its sacrificial beast" (63) must act in such a way that he will deny the dedication of his life to an outsider, Robbie, is a tyrannical imposition on the self. In another, albeit very brief, retelling, Aunt Tempe condones his self-sacrificial gesture as wholly appropriate to the male responsibilities of the Fairchild line (115). Orrin's version, the first in the progression of tellings, so blandly assumes George's actions to be natural as not to comment on them at all. By arranging the various versions of the Yellow Dog episode within this thematic frame, then, the reader can discern a gendered distribution of identity as a theme Welty explores in the novel.

There is more to *Delta Wedding,* however, than the Yellow Dog episode. Another repeated incident, strongly suggestive of the theme of community v. individual, but going beneath it to suggest an unconscious subtext, is the violent confrontation of white man and black in the presence of white female witnesses. Critics who found insufficient attention to southern racial politics in the novel had looked only on the realistic surface. Welty was not defensive about the racial underpinning of southern society.

In the first of two episodes that "bookend" the novel, Dabney, riding out the morning of the wedding rehearsal, recalls an incident from her childhood:

It was a day in childhood, they were living at the Grove. She had wandered off—no older than India now—and had seen George come on a small scuffle, a scuffle with a knife, out in the woods—right here. George, thin, lanky, exultant, "wild," they said smilingly, had been down at the Grove from school that summer. Two of their little Negroes had flown at each other with extraordinary intensity here on the bank of the bayou. It was in the bright sun, in front of the cypress shadows. At the jerk-back of a little wrist, suddenly a knife let loose and seemed to fling itself in the air. Uncle George and Uncle Denis (who was killed the next year in the war) had just come out of the bayou, naked, so wet they shone in the sun, wet light hair hanging over their foreheads just alike, and they were stamping their feet, flinging out their arms, starting to wrestle and to play, and Uncle George reared up and caught the knife. . . . It was a big knife—she was

sure it was as big as the one Troy could pull now. There
was blood on the sunny ground. (35)

Dabney remembers George emerging from the violence as a kind
of apotheosis of racial and sexual splendor. He stills the two
fighting Negro boys, uses his own shirt to bandage the one who
has been cut, then turns to acknowledge Dabney's presence:

When George turned around on the bayou, his face looked
white and his sunburn a mask, and he stood there still and
attentive. There was blood on his hands and both legs. He
stood looking not like a boy close kin to them, but out by
himself, like a man who had stepped outside—done something. But it had not been anything Dabney wanted to see
him do. She almost ran away. He seemed to meditate—to
refuse to smile. She gave a loud scream and he saw her
there in the field, and caught her when she ran at him. He
hugged her tight against his chest, where sweat and bayou
water pressed her mouth, and tickled her a minute, and told
her how sorry he was to have scared her like that. (36)

The scene is a lode of embedded meaning. Sweat, white flesh
carrying the blood of the other race, and bayou water mingle in
George's embrace of the young girl to initiate her (with strong
sexual overtones, since he is naked at the time) into an experience rich almost to confusion with shapings of her (female) character. Desire and fear combine in Dabney's "decision" to bolt
into George's embrace. Her marriage to Troy Flavin eight years

later is a continuation of the headlong rush toward experience which defined her character in the bayou incident.

Troy carries all of the markers of sexuality, race, and violence woven into George's bayou scene. Identified repeatedly by his full head of red hair and the hairs sprouting from the backs of his hands, Troy is a satyr. More often than not on horseback, he is doubly sexualized as a centaur. When his mother sends quilts from Tishomingo County as a wedding present, Troy openly declares "Delectable Mountains" his favorite pattern, and "the one I aim for Dabney and me to sleep under most generally, warm *and* pretty" (113). Aunt Tempe gives Ellen "a long look" at Troy's utterance, as if to underscore his frank admission that he is taking Dabney as a sexual partner.

He is also the designated enforcer of the racial power structure by which Shellmound, the Fairchild plantation, and the agrarian south as a whole, produces wealth. Early in the novel he is seen in plain iconic flatness as an emblem:

A man on a black horse rode across their path at right angles, down Mound Field. He waved, his arm like a gun against the sky—it was Troy on Isabelle. (30)

Battle Fairchild, who has ceded all practical control of the plantation to Troy, lifts himself to the podium of soft-hearted gentleman on the strong and merciless arm of his overseer. Troy makes this amply plain, perhaps so plain as to cause some discomfort to his employers, when he sums up his view of the social transition from hill country to Delta:

"By now, I can't tell a bit of difference between me and any
Delta people you name. There's nothing easy about the
Delta either, but it's just a matter of knowing how to han-
dle your Negroes." (95)

He handles them with his merciless gun-like arm.

In a scene directly reiterating the one Dabney remembers
on the bayou, her sister Shelley encounters Troy on the evening
of the wedding rehearsal. The images of the earlier episode—
blood, racial violence, sexuality—are repeated in Shelley's
encounter:

The green-shaded light fell over the desk. It shone on that
bright-red head. Troy was sitting there—bathed and
dressed in a stiff white suit, but having trouble with some
of the hands. Shelley walked into the point of a knife.

Root M'Hook, a field Negro, held the knife drawn; it
was not actually a knife, it was an ice pick. Juju and
another Negro stood behind with slashed cheeks, and
open-mouthed; still another, talking to himself, stood his
turn apart. (195)

Whereas Dabney's remembered moment of initiation into the
experience of white female adulthood carries an aura of mystery, Shelley's encounter is unmediated. Troy "having trouble
with some of the hands" is all about the exercise of power;
there is no bear hug of reconciliation such as Dabney witnessed:

"You start to throw that at me, I'll shoot you," Troy said.

Root vibrated his arm, aiming. Troy shot the finger of his hand, and Root fell back, crying out and waving at him. (195)

Shelley's encounter pushes her much more overtly into the raw relations of power between the races and sexes. While M'Hook bleeds from the stump of a missing finger, the silent black man, called Big Baby, reveals that his buttocks have been stung full of buckshot. Troy calls for the ice pick and orders Big Baby to drop his pants. He taunts his future sister-in-law with the interracial sexual theme running through southern fiction: "'Shelley, did you come to watch me?'" (196).

Shelley declines, but cannot make an easy exit because there is blood on the door. Troy tells her, mockingly, that she will just have to jump over it. "[S]he could see the reason why Dabney's wedding should be prevented," but Shelley knows she will be powerless to do so (196). What she carries away from the encounter in the overseer's office, though, is a lesson in the superiority of women, not a lesson in the evils of racial oppression:

She felt again, but differently, that men were no better than little children. She ran across the grass toward the house. Women, she was glad to think, did know a *little* better—though everything they knew they would have to keep to themselves . . . oh, forever! (196)

Dabney rushes into the conflicts of life with a headlong earnestness that her older sister cannot match. Whereas Dabney can look into the Yazoo River and stare frankly at its symbolic figures of the sexual and racial unconscious, Shelley glides along its bank framing it in tidy similes: "like the curved arm of the sleeper, whose elbow was in their garden" (123, 194). In Dabney's possession, the glass night-light—gift of the old-maid aunts—is broken before it even gets into the house. For all it represents of physical sanctuary and family memory, Dabney has no tears and apparently no respect for its symbolism (53). In Shelley's mind, Dabney casually walks into something she (Shelley) dreaded (85).

The contrast between the sisters, sown throughout the novel, is drawn into focus by the repetition of episodes of racial, sexual, physical encounter with the "real" circumstances of identity by which the two young women are bound: their race, their sex, their class. Shelley would postpone indefinitely any form of acknowledgment of these constraints. Ellen, her mother, worries that there is "something not quite *warm* about Shelley" (212). Her "ragamuffinism" (212) and affectation of tomboy identity indicates a rejection of the female role her mother and aunts seem to have accepted as natural. In fact, when Shelley directly attacks Battle, her father, for "getting Mama in this predicament [pregnancy]—again and again," (229) she strikes at the physical and ideological system of the Shellmound world. It is such a radical, and direct, attack that Battle cannot understand it.

From the theme of the competing demands of personal and communal identity, *Delta Wedding* merges into the complicated and crowded theme of male and female social and psychological roles. Some glimmer of Welty's credentials in this debate is visible in the earlier mention of Heilbrun's study of Woolf's feminism. Welty absorbed this feminism with the literary form she imported from Woolf's fiction. Men are, by social decree and probably by nature, prone to violence. The sainted Denis died in France in World War I, but even before that he and George rose to their apotheosis in the wounding violence at the bayou. Troy is an extrapolation of that myth-shrouded violence toward the socioeconomic realities of maintaining control over the labor force of a lucrative plantation in the Mississippi Delta. Albert Devlin's book *Eudora Welty's Chronicle: A Story of Mississippi Life* contains a foundational study of structural relationships between Welty's *Delta Wedding* and the tradition of the plantation novel from which it grew.[5]

Violence and honor, integral parts of the plantation legend in fiction and in history, define the dead Fairchild men. Dabney's grandfather had been killed in a duel over cotton and a point of honor that the granddaughter can no longer remember or claim. "To give up your life because you thought that much of your *cotton* — where was love, even, in that? *Other* people's cotton. Fine glory! Dabney would have none of it" (120). Farther back, Fairchild men had made a family tradition of dying by violent means: in the Battle of Shiloh, in a frontier murder.

The tradition of honor and death accumulates on the figure of George Fairchild. George, a lawyer and former "aeronaut" in World War I echoes the suicidally depressive character of Bayard Sartoris in Faulkner's *Flags in the Dust* (1929). He is clearly a thin crust of manners over an abyss of desperation. He is not above the gratuitous act of cruelty. When Ellen reports to him that she has met an unfamiliar white girl in the woods, George retaliates with the claim that he had slept with her in an old cotton gin. "Sometimes," Ellen muses as if to pardon him, "he, the kindest of them all, would say a deliberate wounding thing—as if in assurance that nothing further might then hurt you" (79). Whatever George's reasons for saying the "wounding thing," and whether or not he indeed did sleep with the girl, his words reinforce the theme of men as the wounders, women as the wounded, in a "natural" pageant that has gone this way for decades in the Fairchild family, and in history at large.

Troy is also strongly implicated in this pattern of male violence; as the hill-country interloper, however, his violent behavior carries no patina of honor. He "handles" the black labor with a ruthless efficiency. When he takes over as overseer, for example, he has Battle Fairchild get rid of the more troublesome of the two black boys (now men) whose fight George had refereed in the bayou (36). He is quick to shoot when he feels himself threatened by a black worker, yet speaks tenderly of his little mother in the Tishomingo hills. And, it is not unthinkable that the young white woman whom Ellen meets in the woods bears some connection, perhaps sexual, to Troy, for the only clue to why the strange girl was in the Fairchild woods is that Ellen is "dimly aware [that] the chimney to the overseer's house stuck up through the trees" (69). The phallic chimney is an appropriate emblem for Troy, and Ellen interprets it as such unconsciously: speaking to the strange girl, Ellen pretends she is one of her own daughters (71).

The male characters of *Delta Wedding* share a propensity for violence—physical, psychological, racial. Even Roy, a Peter

Pan-ish youngster, throws Laura into the Yazoo just to see if a girl will float (179). His younger brother Ranny apes his white male elders by ordering the black servant Roxie to bring him coffee in the morning (208). Ellen, the central maternal consciousness of the novel, endures the behavior of men because, as she tries to tell the strange girl in the woods, men are "our [women's] lives" (71). Ellen surely is invested in the mutuality of the male/female relationship. She is a perennially fruitful womb for Battle, but her erotic energies spill over upon George. As she puts him to bed after his long ride on horseback from Memphis, Ellen feasts on the undefended sight of him—as if he were a swashbuckling idol:

> In the darkened room his hair and all looked dark—turbulent and dark, almost Spanish. Spanish! She looked at him tenderly to have thought of such a far-fetched thing, and went out. (51)

Not so far-fetched, though, for at the evening reception after Dabney's wedding, Ellen's eyes follow George through the crowd. When they dance, her surrender to him is a lover's surrender (222–23).

In *Delta Wedding* the women characters run the gamut of nurturers and preservers from fanatic old maid aunts to eager Persephones, from Aunt Primrose and Jim Allen to Dabney. They might not own clear title to the real estate, but they preside over spaces and they preserve the scripts and recipes of ritual that make the family survive over time. An outsider like Robbie Reid, who brings a singular and personal need for love into the clan, has a difficult time against arrayed forces of the status quo. She rails against them, but is eventually reinscribed in the Fairchild book of male and female. Perhaps only Shelley, among the women narrators of the novel, can claim estrangement, distance, analytical detachment. She is, of course, the surrogate of the author of the novel; one of the photographs in her room is a replica of one of Welty herself, dressed up in a campy spoof of romantic Andalusian grandeur (83).[6] Shelley writes the story of Fairchild rather than lives it.

The men are strangers to the women, strangers who brood in Byronic mystery, like George, or in alcoholic befuddlement, like Pinckney Summers. They are Jovian blusterers, like Battle, who huff and puff but eventually do what the women tell them to do. They are satyrs, like Troy, who do the dirty work of labor management and sex. They have died in trials of honor, leaving women to rear children and keep land holdings from disintegrating. Men might even be considered as "different" as the blacks of *Delta Wedding*. One of the temptations of reading *Delta Wedding* is to follow the intricacies of the novel's form so intently as to miss the criticism of southern racial patterns of behavior and the exploration of (and protest against) entrenched gender lines.

As the novel opens with Laura's welcome by the swarming Fairchild cousins, the blacks make their entrance in a way familiar to a thousand plantation novels and the films later to be based on them: they are arrayed as a roster of willing adjuncts to the lifestyle of the plantation. Laura remembers their names (8) and the fact that although they work in the fields and house, they live in "Brunswicktown where the

Negroes were" (6). The Yellow Dog, a train so meek that Mr. Doolittle often stops it to pick goldenrod, nevertheless has a Jim Crow car, although it is not until page 235 that we find out. If Shellmound is a pastoral enclave, held up out of historical circumstance, it is still a segregated one. The friction between the clear intention to keep *Delta Wedding* clear of historical obligations and the inevitability of recognizing racial segregation as the iceberg tip of that history makes for an interesting reading of the novel.

If Dabney is the Persephone figure, the princess of the Shellmound domain offered to a demi-god (Troy) to end the drought, for it is a dry season in which Dabney is wed, she is also (like her avatar Scarlett O'Hara) an imperious enforcer of the prevailing rules of race. When Man-Son, one of the blacks who works in the fields, raises his hat to speak to her, Dabney is shaken. As a boy, Man-Son had been one of the two fighting youths George had separated (36). He is now a young man, perhaps close to Dabney's own age, and she reacts to his declaration of his presence with a kind of trepidation and authoritarian abruptness: "'You get to picking!'" (37).

The tendency of the blacks of Shellmound to interject themselves and their condition into the dream of life maintained by the whites from top to bottom gives certain scenes a deceptive edge. As an enclave withdrawn from history, Shellmound is not perfect. Laura's welcome is underscored by the rhythm of work. As she and her hosts eat cake, "[the] throb of the compress had never stopped. Laura could feel it now in the handle of her cup, the noiseless vibration that trembled in the best china, was within it" (17). Labor value duels with aesthetic value. And it is no secret who does the work. Even in the so-called silence of the early morning at Shellmound, Laura "could hear nothing, except the sounds of the Negroes," the sounds of ongoing work (55). When the fabulous wedding cake arrives from Memphis, black arms and backs haul it into place as the white celebrants of the Delta wedding stand aside. There is a clear divide between celebration of family and work (201).

If the work sounds of the Negroes supply a background hum for the novel, certain black characters are put forward as direct counterpoint to the white. Pinchy, a black girl of the age of Ellen's daughters, appears periodically in the narrative as a shadow to the progress of Dabney toward her wedding. Pinchy is "coming through," locked in an interior struggle—spiritual and psychological, perhaps also physical—the outcome of which is "sanity." As readers get layer upon layer of the memory of the white women trying to reconcile honor and love, past and present, insider and outsider, there is no clue to the interior state of Pinchy's mind. That it might be more than interior is obliquely hinted in the clash between Root M'Hook and Troy Flavin (195).

Dabney's interior preparation for marriage requires a similar "coming through." Visiting her old-maid aunts, she learns that her cousin has just had a baby:

> "Dabney, where were you?" The aunts, with India holding their hands and swinging between them, came in. "Mary Denis Summers Buchanan has come through her ordeal—very well," said Aunt Jim Allen. "Tempe just telephoned from Inverness—didn't you hear us calling you? She wanted us to tell you it was a boy."

"I think Dabney's been eating green apples, but I feel all right," India said. (41–42)

"Coming through" is clearly an initiation in some form that transforms girls into women, women into mothers. It is not to be dismissed lightly, for even Ellen, pregnant for the tenth time, fears her own death in childbirth or complications (226).

Pinchy "comes through" successfully on a timetable very close to Dabney's. On the eve of the wedding she steps into her right mind, and by the day after she is more sane than Aunt Mac Fairchild, who goes to town on a Sunday to pick up the payroll from the bank (203). "Coming through" the ordeal of womanhood throws a bridge between black Pinchy and white Dabney. No doubt but that Dabney faces an ordeal as she contemplates the portrait of the fore-mother Mary Shannon in the parlor of the Grove, the plantation house built around her when the Delta was a frontier (41). Over the years from frontier to early agribusiness, the ordeal has gone inward; coming through is no less important as a restoration of the real to the community white and black.

Delta Wedding is a complex and deceptively mild novel which has proven itself adaptable to changing fashions and viewpoints in criticism. For the formalist critic it offers cyclical patterning, juxtapositions, paralleling, and an intriguing use of symbolism. Welty's manipulation of several different narrative styles for the Yellow Dog episode suggests that the author wants readers to know that *Delta Wedding,* at least in part, is a novel about writing novels. Early reviewers and interpreters located the theme of individual vs. community and have explicated Welty's treatment of competing claims, pros and cons. Feminist readers such as Louise Westling in her *Sacred Groves and Ravished Gardens* have placed *Delta Wedding* prominently high in the rankings of novels that explore the claims of women's fiction to a set-apart language and style.[7] Even historicist critics, those who look for ways to read the script of historical conditions in works that seem immune to history, can find in *Delta Wedding* the traces of what they seek: a kind of materialist critique of the relations of labor and capital, and the necessary fictions of formalized behavior by the latter—a wedding, say—conjured to obliterate all trace of the former. If Eudora Welty was reluctant to write a novel, her first one turned out to be a rich and challenging experience for all of its readers.

CHAPTER FIVE

The Golden Apples

The Golden Apples (1949) is one of the greatest achievements of modernist American literature; it ranks with Faulkner's *The Sound and the Fury* (1929), T. S. Eliot's *The Waste Land* (1922), or the later plays of Eugene O'Neill (especially the family-themed *A Long Day's Journey into Night* [1956]). In the realm of transatlantic literary modernism, *The Golden Apples* merits comparison with the works of Virginia Woolf and Elizabeth Bowen (two of Welty's acknowledged models), as well as with E. M. Forster, D. H. Lawrence, and James Joyce—names Welty herself listed as the foremost writers of modern fiction.

Reviewers of *The Golden Apples* in 1949 were, under-standably, reluctant to make sweeping claims for Welty's book. When "upscale" comparisons were made, the achievement to which Welty's was linked was fellow Mississippi writer William Faulkner. Hamilton Basso, himself a Mississippian, thought Welty to be Faulkner's equal—high praise by any standards. Malcolm Cowley, who had recently compiled *The Portable Faulkner* (1946), also found grounds for a favorable comparison. And Francis Steegmuller, in the *New York Times Book Review,* made comparisons with Twain and Sherwood Anderson.[1]

The querulous reviewers were, ironically, the more constructive, for they often indicated powerful meanings in *The Golden Apples* that critics have eventually explored. Coleman Rosenberger showed fine attention to Welty's technique, but faulted "a quality that is often almost trance-like, and, at its least successful, a little slight and attenuated."[2] "Slightness" and "attenuation" have been reappraised by subsequent feminist readings as considerably more substantial. The reviewer for the *Christian Science Monitor* was harsher; Olive Dean Hormel judged character and place "pervaded by a poisonous miasma. For all their poetry, they chronicle little else than sensualism, perversities, and frustrations."[3] Reviewers who expressed puzzlement or offense at the intricate, associational narrative have been answered many times over by more patient critical studies that have explored the modernist method in *The Golden Apples,* and the alleged "sensualism" has been reinterpreted by feminist critics as a system of intuition rather than analytic logic.

There are several reasons why *The Golden Apples* deserves this ranking and the critical attention that goes with it. First, there is Welty's command of the modernist technique of using myth (classical, Celtic, American folk, and others) to give form to a diverse cast of characters engaged in a complex network of interaction. "These fragments I shore against my ruin," Eliot wrote, and his line has become the motto for all modernist writers. In *The Sound and the Fury,* Faulkner uses the Christian narrative of death and resurrection to create coherence (tonal and structural) in a work that is fundamentally about incoherence—in personality, in memory, in family, in history. *The Waste Land* is, by critical consensus, the standard case for the use of the mythic method, for Eliot uses Christian, classical, Oriental, and primitive myths, more or less as they were digested in Sir James Frazer's *The Golden Bough*

(1890–1915). Joyce takes the trophy for the consistent use of classical myth in a modernist novel for *Ulysses.*

Welty was sharply aware of her "competition," the roster of precursors who, in decades just preceding her debut as a writer in the mid-1930s, had set the course she chose to follow. Welty knew the mythology she used in *The Golden Apples:*

> It is conscious [the use of mythology], clearly. I've lived with mythology all my life. It is just as close to me as the landscape. It *naturally* occurs to me when I am writing fiction. It is not a far-out, reached-for something. I feel no sense of strain when I use mythology.[4]

Anticipating her interviewer's direction, Welty softly deflects one of the formulaic approaches to modernist literature: the tendency to read text and myth in a one-to-one inflexible relationship. Welty explains: "But I think that anyone who attributes my stories to myths very specifically and thoroughly is overshooting it. I would rather suggest things" (224).

Another identifying mark of the modernist, discussed in chapter 4, is the fragmentation of realistic time and, consequently, of narrative, followed by the reassembling of it by means other than chronology. Welty had found the technique of dissociative narration in Woolf and turned it to her purposes in *Delta Wedding.* The composition and publishing history of the individual stories of *The Golden Apples* sheds additional light on this aspect of Welty's evolving technique.

"The Whole World Knows," Randall MacLain's Faulknerian monologue, was the first of the seven stories to be written and circulated to magazines. "June Recital," under the title "Golden Apples," was drafted at about the same time, in the autumn of 1946. A year and a half elapsed before "Shower of Gold" and "Sir Rabbit" were completed. While revising "Music from Spain" in San Francisco in 1948, Welty had the insight that the separate stories were in fact related by place and character. She then revised them all—especially "Sir Rabbit"—and completed the final two longer stories, "The Wanderers" (published in *Harper's Bazaar* as "The Hummingbirds") and "Moon Lake" as parts of the ensemble. When assembled for *The Golden Apples* the stories were placed in chronological order. Moreover, Welty took a lesson from Hemingway's *In Our Time* (1925) by alternating shorter and longer stories in her collection, using the shorter to suggest bits of character, the passing of time, and connective tissue in patterns of imagery which are then enhanced in the longer stories.

As literary modernism declines to accept the unity of narrative according to the historical model, it also questions the unity of personality. Modern physics had done much to change the popular sense of the solidity of matter and the symmetry of time. Freud and Jung had all but demolished the model of the unified and consciously monitored personality. The self the modernists knew was a sometimes noisy parliament of avatars and archetypes, ids, egos, and superegos. The individual dissolved into wide categories of human experience spread over time and space. Eliot's alienated speaker in *The Waste Land* shares his identity with Jesus Christ through the mediation of the Fisher King. Faulkner's Compson brothers (Benjy, Quentin, and Jason) are near-textbook examples of id, superego, and ego. Welty's central fugitive in *The Golden Apples,* King

MacLain—randy, insatiable, indomitable, and cruel—is a masculinized archetype of irresponsible libido. King will not stop until, as his grandson and namesake says, he pops (229). From character to archetype, Welty plots King through various facets of "meaning, evoking classical mythology, psychoanalytic versions of the burden of the Father, and Mississippi history." Multileveled conceptions of literary character require multileveled readerly attention. The modernist work is difficult by design. For an excellent introduction for this kind of reading of *The Golden Apples,* see Thomas McHaney's "Eudora Welty and the Multitudinous Golden Apples."

Modernist literature is extremely conscious of itself as part of a literary discourse; readers should never mistake what is told for actual reality. That is, the modernist text knows itself to be a text—something made—and not a transparent "window on life." Modernist self-consciousness manifests itself in several ways. One way is understanding the fundamentals of narrative fiction (character and plot) as representing more than one meaning and performing more than one function. King MacLain, for example, figures Zeus and the historical personage of James K. Vardaman. Another way modernist literary self-consciousness is satisfied is by calling attention to itself *as writing.* On perhaps the most accessible level this is evident in quotation or allusion. Welty, for example, has her character Cassie Morrison recall a few lines from "The Song of Wandering Aengus" by William Butler Yeats—but neither Welty nor Cassie names Yeats. Yeats's poem then lends images to *The Golden Apples.* Morgana is not just a small town in Mississippi, but a field upon which a literary performance is staged.

Yet another manifestation of literary performance is the aside or passage of imitation or parody. In "Moon Lake," for example, Welty situates Loch Morrison, "the Boy Scout," as a character and herself as a female southern author in relation to William Faulkner's Joe Christmas, the central character of *Light in August* (1932). Christmas's notorious misogyny is inflicted on his foster mother, Mrs. McEachern, by his refusal to eat the food she has prepared for him:

> He was just eight then. It was years later that memory knew what he was remembering; years later after that night when, an hour later, he rose from the bed and went and knelt in the corner as he had not knelt on the rug [to pray with McEachern], and above the outraged food kneeling, with his hands ate, like a savage, like a dog.[5]

Welty's Loch is a misogynist too, but her response to Faulkner is to soften his assault upon the feminine with parody:

> He [Loch] came and got his food and turned his back and ate it all alone and like a dog and lived in a tent by himself, apart like a nigger, and dived alone when the lake was clear of girls. (100)

The modernist (and southern) Welty positions *The Golden Apples* strategically *as literature* by a steady but not overwhelming use of allusion, quotation, and parodic aside.

Even though Welty has repeatedly said that writing *The Golden Apples* is one of her happiest memories, there are dark strands woven into the stories, dark strands of reaction against misogyny, of anguish within a network of female roles that seem to all but one of her female characters suffocating, and of deep-seated ambivalence about one of her perennially affirmed values: rootedness to place. As exciting as it is to see *The Golden Apples* becoming a whole through the layering and repetition of image, symbol, allusion, and trope, it is just as exciting to see the countervailing forces of negation and questioning at nearly every stage.

The Golden Apples opens with "Shower of Gold." Functioning as the overture to the collection, "Shower of Gold" introduces literary raw materials to be developed in subsequent stories. Katie Rainey, a poor white woman living in Morgana, Mississippi, Welty's imagined Delta town, has the podium, narrating the story of Snowdie Hudson and King MacLain, the "first parents" of the developing story. Snowdie, an albino, is the daughter of a store-keeper in Morgana, so it is doubly surprising to one and all that King MacLain, a socially prominent bachelor—echoing Don McInnis of "Asphodel"—chooses Snowdie to be his wife. The Hudson/MacLain marriage is not so much the partnering of two persons as the linking of diametrically opposed forms of being: one female, the other male. Snowdie, Katie reports, had been tagged as an old maid early: "And I guess people more or less expected her to teach school: not marry" (5). In her wedding dress, Snowdie clearly mirrors a Jungian archetype, the anima or transcendence of material in the female figure: "And once they dressed Snowdie all in white, you know she was whiter than your dreams" (5).

King, on the other hand, is the incarnation (in the male body) of the hit-and-run principle of self-satisfaction without responsibility. No sooner does he marry Snowdie than he begins his mysterious shape-shifting and constant travel: "He sold tea and spices," Katie remembers (7), and so is admitted to a club of Marco Polos, male figures whose preference is to remain untied and on the move. King returns home periodically to impregnate one woman or another; Katie will not say whom, though she obviously has her suspicions. When it is Snowdie, her annunciation—the moment in which she tells Katie that she is expecting a child—is decorated by the classical myth of Zeus and Danae:

She looks like more than only the news had come over her. It was like a shower of something had struck her, like she'd been caught out in something bright. It was more than the day. (6)

It was in the form of a shower of gold that Zeus raped the nymph Danae. Using the classical image, therefore, does not only establish the connection between the text of Welty's story and the text of the myth beyond it, it also connects antithetical acts or figures: rape and the bestowal of gift, for example.

Having met his wife, and undisclosed additional partners (perhaps Katie herself, for she seems to know a lot about the trysting place [5]), King departs. He is seen, as befits a mythic figure, all over, and is known by his emblems: wide-brimmed hats and flowing locks. He is reported in Texas, for example, getting a haircut. But King is also sighted in history as well as in myth. One sighting in particular alerts us that history is also subject to mythic representation. The sighting of King at the inauguration of Gov. James K. Vardaman, in Jackson, Mississippi, in 1904, both dates the beginning of *The Golden Apples* and introduces a historical theme—southern racism, particularly the violent and sexually hysterical brand of racism practiced by Vardaman in his election campaigns. The historical James Kemble Vardaman (1861–1930), governor of Mississippi 1904–08 and U.S. Senator 1913–19, functions as complement to the mythic meanings of King as local Zeus. And the chief deity of Olympus is set down a peg by being embodied in a redneck racist.

Anticipating more modern public relations strategies, Vardaman attired himself in wide-brimmed hats and a white frock coat while campaigning and governing, and his flowing hair contributed to his emblematic appearance. He was called the Great White Chief. As a racist demagogue, Vardaman openly suggested lynching to keep the African American population in fear and submission; when Vardaman spoke "rape" he did not mean showers of gold or encounters with swans. If King's associations intersect with those of Zeus on the putatively positive range of cultural acceptability, they also delve into the repugnant as they cross Vardaman's. This textual tension undercuts blithe approval of King and his escapades and keeps readers at least subliminally conscious of historical place and time as the text operates on the level of myth.

King's next visit, also reported by Katie, is his Halloween encounter with his twin sons, Eugene (masked as a Chinaman) and Lucius Randall (masked as a lady). King takes one look at his offspring and beats a hasty exit, leaving his trademark hat on the banks of the Big Black River. Perhaps King knows something his wife as yet does not suspect. Born on January 1 (8), the twins were conceived (in literary computation of time) on April 1. If their conception was a joke on Snowdie, King's encounter with them steers the joke back to him. He scrams. Snowdie never sees her husband on this trip. She believes King was in the vicinity, however, on the testimony of an old black man who knows everyone in and around Morgana. And Plez Morgan, the black man, knows King not because he has seen his face, but because he has read his signs: his stride, his wide-brimmed hat, and, most importantly for the gesture system of *The Golden Apples,* by the stance King strikes as he pauses outside his own front door, eavesdropping:

> So Plez says presently the familiar stranger paused. It was in front of the MacLains'—and sunk his weight on one leg and just stood there, posey as statues, hand on his hip. (12)

As *The Golden Apples* progresses, this pose becomes telling. King's posture is the posture of Perseus, the child conceived by Danae, whose greatest exploit was displaying the head of Medusa in the "vaunting" posture of the triumphant male holding as trophy the severed head of the female. Deployed in the initial story, still awaiting its repetitions, this image illustrates one of the crucial disciplines of the modernist text: its reversibility. In traditional narrative, narrative determined by the observed "facts" of human experience in time and place, events occur once in the temporal sequence; an event happening earlier in the sequence cannot mean in its time what an event occurring later might suggest. The modernist plot abolishes this restriction. The plot of *The Golden Apples* continually surprises the reader with the intricacy of its reversible currents of connection.

"Shower of Gold" functions as well as entertains. In the story that launches *The Golden Apples* Welty establishes just enough plot to web the events to a discernible history in time and place, the Mississippi Delta at the turn of the century and, more specifically, in the political administration of James K. Vardaman. She gives some detail for the myriad names in her list of characters. She initiates the usage of an intertextual system of reference to classical Greek and Roman mythology. She sketches the beginnings of the themes of male and female cross-purposes and of racial antagonism. She uses a narrator, Katie Rainey, who knows more than she tells. Adding the embedded foreshadowings of events in the following stories, "Shower of Gold" functions admirably on its own and as a literary overture to the rest of the whole of which it is a part.

"June Recital" moves the present moment of *The Golden Apples* forward sixteen years; it is about 1920. Virgie Rainey, who had been but a baby in "Shower of Gold," is now sixteen (21). She is a restless and risk-taking teenager with a sailor boyfriend with whom she keeps rendezvous in the MacLain house, now deserted. Virgie is first spied there by Loch Morrison, confined to bed with malaria but just as restless and risk-taking as Virgie. Loch climbs out of his bedroom-prison on the limbs of a hackberry tree and dangles by his feet as he eavesdrops on the events that transpire in the vacant house. He is too young to understand half of what he witnesses.

First, Loch sees Virgie and her boyfriend steal into the rear door of the MacLain house and appear in an upstairs bedroom. To get a better view, Loch aims his telescope on the pair:

He moved his eye upstairs, up an inch on the telescope. There on a mattress delightfully bare—where he would love, himself, to lie, on a slant and naked, to let the little cottony tufts annoy him and to feel the mattress like billows bouncing beneath, and to eat pickles lying on his back—the sailor and the piano player [Virgie] lay and ate pickles out of an open sack between them. Because of the down-tilt of the mattress, the girl had to keep watch on the sack, and when it began to slide down out of reach that was when they laughed. Sometimes they held pickles stuck in their mouths like cigars, and turned to look at each other. Sometimes they lay just alike, their legs in an M and their hands joined between them, exactly like the paper dolls his sister used to cut out of folded newspaper and unfold to let him see. If Cassie [his sister] would come in now, he would point out the window and she would remember.

And then, like the paper dolls sprung back together, they folded close—the real people. Like a big grasshopper lighting, all their legs and arms drew into one small body, deadlike, with protective coloring. (26)

This quotation serves multiple purposes. Although it establishes Loch as our eyepiece on the scene, he is only a limited witness, for he cannot name the act of intercourse he sees. In the gap between what Loch sees and what he can name, readers must make *The Golden Apples.*

If the modernist technique of enlisting the reader as the co-maker of the reading experience and its meaning has an annoying feature, it is that sometimes that technique overdetermines our response. In the quoted passage, we are first given one clearly phallic symbol, the pickles. Adding cigars, a phallic symbol so obviously suggesting the godfather of phallic stogies, Sigmund Freud—is excessive. Or perhaps the doubled symbols are an indication of literary play: what is to be remarked is not "what" the characters are doing but, rather, the number of ways we have of telling it.

The latter alternative has possibilities, for the censorship of the erotic by the official norm is a central theme in "June Recital." Loch is clearly on the side of pleasure, as is Virgie. He can imagine a palpable pleasure in his bare skin against the bare mattress that must be, in the passage quoted above, the counterpart to the erotic pleasure that Virgie at least hopes for in making love with the sailor. In the other camp, those who police physical pleasure, is Loch's sister, Cassie. Cassie is looking forward to college in the fall, while Virgie plays piano at the local cinema. Virgie is out in the world; Cassie is behind the locked door of her bedroom. She is turning into something that frightens even herself:

> Cassie saw herself without even facing the mirror, for her small, solemn, unprotected figure was emerging staring-clear inside her mind. There she was now, standing scared at the window again in her petticoat, a little of

each color of the rainbow dropped on her—bodice and
flounce—in spite of reasonable care. Her pale hair was
covered and burdened with twisty papers, like a hat too
big for her. She balanced her head on her frail neck. She
was holding a spoon [for tie-dyeing] up like a mean
switch in her right hand, and her feet were bare. She had
seemed to be favored and happy and she stood there
pathetic—homeless-looking—horrible. (33)

Cassie is becoming Medusa before her own eyes, the horrible
face and hair of serpents that turns pleasurable flesh to stone.

Cassie and Virgie are irreconcilable opposites, like the
Fairchild sisters Dabney and Shelley in *Delta Wedding*. Virgie
ventures ahead, taking risks life presents, while Cassie protects
her chances behind the warning sign on her bedroom door:
"'Everybody stay out!!!'" (32). The relationship between the
two as girls and young women, and as representations of meaning in the story, is worked out in flashbacks to the music
lessons and recital the two had shared as students of Miss Eckhart, a German émigré who turned up in Morgana just before
the First World War. Miss Eckhart brings the two young
women an ominous foreshadowing of their own possibilities as
daughters and women. When her own mother interrupts a lesson by mockingly repeating Miss Eckhart's signal to Virgie
that the pupil has played well, "'Virgie Rainey, *danke shoen,*'"
she calmly slaps her mother in the mouth. Cassie, shocked
beyond understanding (like her younger brother witnessing
sexual intercourse), thought "that it must, after all, have been
the mother that slapped the daughter" (55).

Cassie is, as "June Recital" and the finale, "The Wanderers," make clear, unable to separate from her mother. Mrs. Morrison is not in the least unwilling to live her own life separate from her daughter. When Cassie is daubed with the colors of her tie-dyeing, Mrs. Morrison will not let herself be touched (32). At summer political "speakings" Mrs. Morrison slips away. Cassie always "lost her mother" on such occasions, and when asked Mrs. Morrison would only answer, cryptically, that she had "'just been through yonder to speak to my candidate'" (47).

Mrs. Morrison's alliance with the world of pleasure beyond the policed circle of organized society—"through yonder"—is illustrated by her reaction to the behavior of one Mr. Voight, a bachelor boarder at the MacLain house who exposed himself to the young girls (and one boy: Eugene MacLain) taking piano lessons: "When he flapped his maroon-colored bathrobe, he wore no clothes at all underneath" (42). Cassie can get no adults to believe her story or validate her sense of violation. Her father simply refuses to believe her, and her mother laughs: "'Live and let live, Cassie,' her mother said, meaning it mischievously" (43). Mr. Voight is often misidentified by other Morgana residents as King MacLain (75). And Mrs. Morrison might be one of his partners; Loch's Perseid behavior clearly does not come from Mr. Morrison, father of record.

Miss Eckhart's example to the two young girls comes to a climax one morning as a fierce electrical storm interrupts the lesson. Miss Eckhart seizes the moment and the piano and empties herself in the passionate playing of a piece that bears no relationship to the notes on the page. Miss Eckhart's ecstasy is "too much for Cassie Morrison" (50). It is part of Miss Eckhart's troubling life: on the one hand the ecstasy of her music, on the other the trauma of being raped by "a crazy nigger" (50). Miss Eckhart had not left Morgana after the attack, thereby sticking in the eye of the community an indictment of its own racist hysteria. Morgana drifted away from Miss Eckhart after her rape; and the First World War only abetted their ostracization of the German.

The repressed returns, however, for the old woman whom Loch sees in the vacant Morrison house at the beginning of "June Recital" is identified as Miss Eckhart, an escapee from the asylum. She has returned to the site of her passion and her trauma, intending to burn it down, but she fails. She endures in shame, walking the gauntlet of the assembled ladies of the town. Their card party over, they have come into the street to see the comedy of the nonburning house. The Morgana ladies get an extra: Virgie Rainey is also flushed from the house and walks past them after her lover flees, too, in public. The two most passionate human beings in Morgana are united in a ceremony of shame at the conclusion to "June Recital," yet the momentum of the narrative comes to rest with Cassie, on whom the moment is lost. Cassie remembers Yeats's poem "The Song of the Wandering Aengus," but possibilities of meaning pass beyond her reach:

> All of it passed through her head, through her body. She slept, but sat up in bed once and said aloud, *"Because a fire was in my head."* Then she fell back unresisting. She did not see except in dreams that a face looked in; that it was the grave, unappeased, and radiant face, once more and always, the face that was in the poem. (85)

The dream face also corresponds to the face of King MacLain, unappeased and perhaps unappeasable, the face of the ever-wandering appetite for life.

"Sir Rabbit," the third story in the collection, is a short interlude. Mattie Will Holifield (née Sojourner) remembers a time when she was a girl and the MacLain twins were adolescent boys. Together Ran and Eugene had jumped Mattie Will and rolled her on the ground. Whether any sexual assault took place is doubtful. Mattie Will remembers this earlier encounter with the sons of King when she is out hunting in Morgan's woods with her husband, Junior Holifield, and their black servant. The real King shows up, as he is wont to do, bullies her husband into a faint, then engages Mattie in a semi-willing encounter. She tells the black servant to turn his back and pick some plums when it becomes clear to her what King intends to do:

But he put on her, with the affront of his body, the affront of his sense too. No pleasure in that! She had to put on what he knew with what he did—maybe because he was so grand it was a thorn to him. Like submitting to another way to talk, she could answer to his burden now, his whole blithe, smiling, superior, frantic existence. And no matter what happened to her, she had to remember, disappointments were not to be borne by Mr. MacLain, or he'll go away again.

Now he clasped her to his shoulder, and her tongue tasted sweet starch for the last time. Her arms dropped back to the mossiness, and she was Mr. MacLain's Doom, or Mr. MacLain's Weakness, like the rest, and

neither Mrs. Junior Holifield nor Mattie Will Sojourner;
now she was something she had always heard of. She did
not stir. (95)

When King decamps, a dove's feather, linking this rape with
the story of Leda and the swan, "came turning down through
the light that was like golden smoke" (95).

Whatever her experience with King, it leaves Mattie Will
prouder and more satisfied than her marriage to the common
Junior Holifield. "Sir Rabbit" seems to perform a correction on
the course of King's character, for he had come through the Mr.
Voight incarnation swerving to the criminal. In "June Recital"
the male is either predator or ineffectual: Mr. Voight, the
unnamed black man who rapes Miss Eckhart, on the one side;
Mr. Sissum, who dies or commits suicide before his relationship with Miss Eckhart amounts to much, Mr. Morrison himself probably a cuckold, on the other. The sexual appropriation
of Mattie Will by King is treated as harmless. Coming upon
him in a postcoital sleep, Mattie regains stature. She spies King
almost coatless, almost hatless (96–97). Her own comfort in
reversing the politics of gazer and object is implicit in the lux-
uriant ease of her body as she runs her eyes over the sleeping
man. She is like a cat stretching after a good nap, or a temptress
ready for another go:

Mattie Will subsided forward onto her arms. Her rear
stayed up in the sky, which seemed to brush it with little
feathers. She lay there and listened to the world go round.
(97)

King, blustering to make Mattie Will leave, falls a peg or two from Zeus to a caricature of an old man.

Echoes from earlier stories build up in the fourth story, "Moon Lake." Loch Morrison returns; he is now in his early teenage years and serving as "Boy Scout and Life Saver" to a group of Morgana girls, most of them orphans, at summer camp on Moon Lake. The time-present of the story is the mid-1920s, at least five years on from the time of "June Recital." Although the historical time line is not prominent in the stories, indications of chronological development continue to be present. It is crucial for the reader to take them into account, for repetitions of gesture, language, and image are calibrated to the advancing ages of the characters.

Loch has been "roped into" serving as life guard for the girls by his mother (99). The advancing image of masculinity, running through the various sightings of King and his supporting cast of males, funnels into Loch in "Moon Lake." Welty, using the arch attitudes of some of the teenage town girls (Jinny Love Stark and Nina Carmichael), places Loch against strong images of empty male posturing. For example, Loch blows into his bugle each morning and evening, announcing the beginning and the end of the day. Loch's literal bugle echoes his father's daily newspaper, *The Bugle,* which determined the day of a larger population and, presumably, with more genuine authority. But Loch's expertise with his bugle seems vitiated—at least in a comparison with Mr. Morrison's sense of his own importance to Morgana:

From the beginning his martyred presence seriously affected them. They had a disquieting familiarity with it,

hearing the spit of his despising that went into his bugle.
At times they could hardly recognize what he thought he
was playing. Loch Morrison, Boy Scout and Life Saver,
was under the ordeal of a week's camp on Moon Lake
with girls. (99)

Taking into account the accumulating thematic representation
of the relation (or lack of relation) between the sexes in *The
Golden Apples,* the presentation of Loch as a St. Stephen rid-
dled with arrows of misfortune by being "roped" to girls is
ironic. Loch's clumsiness with the phallic bugle takes on similar ironic resonance. To finish off Loch, Welty puts him up
against a cartoonish macho image, dropping his claim to
importance to the status of a pint-sized Tarzan:

He hardly spoke; he never spoke first. Sometimes he
swung in the trees; Nina Carmichael in particular would
hear him crashing in the foliage somewhere when she
was lying rigid in siesta. (99)

As Loch is determined by his performance, against an ironic
background, of rituals of masculinity, the female characters
of the story are defined by a more supple negotiation with
gendered identity. The "girls" of the Moon Lake camp, it is
crucial to keep in mind, are pushing puberty. As they become
conscious of themselves in a gendered human world, that
world becomes aware of them. Easter, the orphan girl who
focuses so much of Jinny's and Nina's attention, represents
emergent female sexuality. It is obvious, as the text of

"Moon Lake" makes clear, that Easter is one of the by-blows of King's periodic visits to Morgana. She sprouts his trademark hair, "a withstanding gold," and his willful self-determination:

> They [Morgana girls] liked to walk behind her and see her back, which seemed spectacular from crested gold head to hard, tough heel. Mr. Nesbitt, from the Bible Class, took Easter by the wrist and turned her around to him and looked hard at her front. She had started her breasts. What Easter did was to bite his right hand, his collection hand. (105)

Manipulating the women of Morgana is a habit Mr. Nesbitt never breaks; in the final story, "The Wanderers," he has clearly moved from physical manipulation to psychological.

Easter is a female in King's mold; her obliviousness to circumstance (Mr. Nesbitt's attempt to fondle her, the hard facts of her life as an orphan) makes her the target of envy and honor for Jinny and Nina, respectively.

> Easter's eyes, lifting up, were neither brown nor green nor cat; they had something of metal, flat ancient metal, so that you could not see into them. Nina's grandfather had possessed a box of coins from Greece and Rome. Easter's eyes could have come from Greece or Rome that day. Jinny Love stopped short of apprehending this, and only took care to watch herself when Easter pitched the knife [in a game of mumblety-peg]. (106)

The trio of girls constitutes a select range of alternatives in the change from girl to woman. Jinny is unredeemed vulgarity. As a younger girl taking piano lessons from Miss Eckhart in "June Recital" she had a small part, but enough to identify her as a sycophant. In "Moon Lake" she plays "cheerfully" into the scheme of the Vardaman-inspired racial-sexual hysteria—an ideological prison for both black men and white women. On an expedition to Moon Lake without adult counselors, Jinny pipes up with the ideologically correct paranoia: "'I hope we don't meet any nigger men,' Jinny Love said cheerfully" (111).

Nina Carmichael, by comparison, is a more problematic female figure. Nina connects more directly than Jinny, and through her imagination, with the host of representations alive in Easter. When the three girls reach Moon Lake and find an abandoned rowboat, Nina is anxious for a voyage. That there are no oars onboard does not trouble her. But she is deeply frustrated when, as the boat rocks outward on Moon Lake, a chain they had not seen stops their adventure (116). A fuller range of meaning keyed to this incident is opened a few pages later. Evening has fallen and the girls are, except for Nina, asleep. Nina freely indulges her imaginative desire to know the secret of Easter's being: "The orphan! she thought exultantly. The other way to live" (123). "The other way" is clearly, as Welty's text reveals, a way that is open to being touched by the world: raped. The image of rape—written in several connotative registers in the previous (and subsequent) stories in *The Golden Apples*—suggests to Nina a readiness to accept life's risk and fulfillment. In this respect, Nina can be seen verging upon the (gendered) life that Virgie had seized in "June Recital."

The passage in which Nina makes herself available for this life is lengthy, but rich with Welty's language, gesture, image:

Nina sat up on the cot and stared passionately before her at the night—the pale dark roaring night with its secret step, the Indian night. She felt the forehead, the beaded stars, look in thoughtfully at her.

The pondering night stood rude at the tent door, the opening fold would let it stoop in—it, him—he had risen up inside. Long-armed, or long-winged, he stood in the center there where the pole went up. Nina lay back, drawn quietly from him. But the night knew about Easter. All about her. Geneva had pushed her to the very edge of the cot. Easter's hand hung down, opened outward. Come here, night, Easter might say, tender to a giant, to such a dark thing. And the night, obedient and graceful, would kneel to her. Easter's calloused hand hung open there to the night that had got wholly into the tent.

Nina let her own arm stretch forward opposite Easter's. Her hand too opened, of itself. She lay there long time motionless, under the night's gaze, its black cheek, looking immovably at her hand, the only part of her now which was not asleep. (123)

What Jinny Love had parroted in her jejune fear of rape, Nina sees mystically as a female response to phallic rising-standing-poling up. The dark, black, Indian, masculine night is the agent of the other way to be, almost the necessary counterpart to Nina's incompleteness.

"Moon Lake" returns to the trope of the sleeping female and the intrusion of the foreign male in its prolonged denouement. Easter, in spite of having a tough heel, is tickled there and falls (or leaps) into Moon Lake. The girls and counselors are breathless; they know Easter cannot swim. Excited calls go forth for the Boy Scout and lifesaver. Loch springs into action, diving repeatedly into the lake until he grasps Easter by her crest of hair. She is not breathing. Loch flings Easter on her stomach on a picnic table. As Easter's arm dangles, the image so powerful to the sleepless Nina is repeated. Applying artificial respiration, Loch seems to be raping Easter violently while all the girls and adult women counselors watch (127–29).

Jinny Love's mother, Miss Lizzie Stark, drives up in her electric car bringing, as does Miss Sabina in "Asphodel," the strong aroma of female antipathy to pleasure. In her shocked reaction to the scene on the picnic table, readers understand its powerful symbolic meaning:

Miss Lizzie, whose hands were on Nina's shoulders, shook Nina. "Jinny Love Stark, come here to me, Loch Morrison, get off that table and shame on you."

Miss Moody was the one brought to tears. She walked up to Miss Lizzie holding a towel in front of her breast and weeping. "He's our life saver, Miss Lizzie. Remember? Our Boy Scout. Oh, mercy, I'm thankful you've come, he's been doing that a long time. Stand in the shade, Miss Lizzie."

"Boy Scout? Why, he ought to be—he ought to be—I can't stand it, Parnell Moody."

"Can't any of us help it, Miss Lizzie. Can't any of us. It's what he came for." She wept. (130)

Since the "us" Parnell Moody refers to is the exclusively female group of campers and counselors, her words assume a thematic resonance. The mimicking of heterosexual intercourse, exposing by bodily positions the power relations of male and female, rivets the group of girls and women into a corps, and Miss Lizzie speaks for the desire to reject it all.

While Loch works on Easter, another male arrives—Ran MacLain, now twenty-three—with gun and dogs. As he joins the watchers, Loch becomes even more possessive of Easter's body and violent in his "lifesaving" tactics. "The Boy Scout crushed in her body and blood came out of her mouth. For them all, it was like being spoken to" (133). Parnell Moody, for cryptic motives possibly suggested by what is transpiring on the picnic table, addresses the newcomer: "'Oh, Ran. How could you? Oh, Ran'" (133).

As the symbol system fills out, Easter is revived, Ran departs, and the routine of the camp is resumed. The meanings let loose in the story, however, attach themselves to the fundamental pattern of female emergence into a gendered adult world that seems to demand her surrender of autonomy. Jinny and Nina wander down to Loch's tent after nightfall. But this scene of masculine hero, tent, night, and female waiting—unlike the one in which Nina approaches epiphany—is determined by Jinny Love's point of view. Imitating her mother, Jinny Love mocks the male:

> He was naked and there was his little tickling thing hung
> on him like the last drop on the pitcher's lip. He ceased
> or exhausted study and came to the tent opening again
> and stood leaning on one raised arm, with his weight on
> one foot—just looking out into the night, which was
> clamorous. (138)

Jinny Love has the last word: "'You and I will always be old maids,' she added" (138).

Jinny Love is not, as subsequent stories reveal, a reliable prophetess. Both she and Nina are eventually married, and Jinny to Ran MacLain, in spite of the context of their "meeting" at the "rape" of Easter. But Jinny's is a revealing point of view on the recurring cluster of image, language, and gesture that Welty uses to "quilt" the several stories of *The Golden Apples* into one text. Loch's pose, repeating King's (his father's?) pose in "Shower of Gold," repeats as well the sculpted pose of Perseus displaying the severed head of Medusa. Through an earlier story and outward to Greek and Roman mythology, this gesture draws the parts of the collection into a whole. The whole congregates on the theme of male and female interrelations, assumptions of possession and autonomy on the part of the male, resistance to or evasion of the same by the female expressed in a range of motifs and images drawn from popular entertainment (*The Sheik*) and reconciled with Mississippi racial politics (Vardamanic rape and lynch hysteria), more general cultural archetype (Snowdie as Jungian anima), and homemade symbol (the dangling, open hand). More than the elements of classical mythology came together for Welty in *The Golden Apples*.

THE GOLDEN APPLES

"The Whole World Knows," like "Shower of Gold" a dramatic monologue, is starkly unlike its predecessor in that the free-range sexual appetite of King that Katie Rainey condones in the first story—refusing to indict King for his peripatetic ways and absent father/husband performance—recoils on Ran MacLain as waves of guilt. He is married to Jinny Love Stark, but estranged. She retaliates with an affair with a younger man. Ran escalates by initiating an affair with a still younger country woman, Maideen Sumrall. He takes Maideen to a speakeasy moored off the riverbank in Vicksburg, then to a motel. All the while, Ran's monologue is directed to his absent father and to Snowdie, his mother. A deep psychological and sexual hurt drives him to vengeance, and Maideen is the innocent victim (a less resilient Mattie Will, to whom she is related in the Sojourner family tree).

Ran's twisted vengeance reveals the male, which sex by this point in the narrative he represents, to be fundamentally sadomasochistic in addition to its other flaws. In a darkened motel room, Ran takes out a pistol (yet another phallic symbol) and warns Maideen away from the bed. She tries to soothe him out of his despair, but he taunts her further by putting the pistol barrel into his mouth. The way Welty describes Ran's move gives it an auto-erotic frisson: "I put the pistol's mouth to my own" (160). Ran's suicidal but theatrical gesture turns darkly misogynistic:

She took it [the pistol] from me. Dainty as she always was, she carried it over to the chair; and prissy as she was, like she knew some long-tried way to deal with a

gun, she folded it in her dress. She came back to the bed
again, and dropped down on it.

In a minute she put her hand out again, differently,
and laid it cold on my shoulder. And I had her so quick.
(160)

Ran's sexual predation fails of even the semblance of the *joie
de vivre* that, arguably, justifies his father's serial comman-
deering of women. Ran's rape of Maideen is indeed criminal,
for the victim commits suicide. Unlike her Sojourner
kinswoman, who "skedaddled" when King bade her do so (97),
Maideen took her loss to heart.

As "The Whole World Knows" ends with a scene of violence typifying the relations of the sexes, "Music from Spain"
opens with Ran's exiled brother, Eugene, living in San Francisco, striking his wife, Emma, at breakfast. His motivation is
nebulous, long-standing, cumulative. He is in his forties, which
sets the time of the story in the post–World War II years, and
his wife is slightly older and looking her age (161). The misogynistic annoyance that Ran felt at Maideen's behavior is, for
Eugene, simple hostility to his wife's aging looks. She is "fat,
at least plump," and the bodily engulfing this flesh represents
engenders fear and loathing in Eugene. "*He struck her because
he wanted another love*" (164).

The slap on the face functions like a slap on the behind to
Eugene, and he goes out into the San Francisco world as if
newborn. He skips his job at a jeweler's, where he takes care of
time by repairing watches, and wanders the streets not knowing
what other love he seeks. It must be intimacy, though, such as

he has never had with Emma, or has lost since the death of their only daughter, Fan, a year earlier:

> A small Chinese girl, all by herself, with her hair up in aluminum curlers, went around Eugene, swinging a little silky purse. He all but put out a staying hand. When a stocky boy with a black pompadour went by him wearing taps on his shoes, some word waited unspoken on Eugene's lips. His chance for speaking tapped rhythmically by. He frowned in the street, the more tantalized, somehow, by seeing at the last minute that the stranger was tattooed with a butterfly on the inner side of his wrist; an intimate place, the wrist appeared to be. Eugene saw the butterfly plainly enough to recognize it again, when this unfamiliar, calloused hand of San Francisco put a flame to a bitten cigarette. (169)

The small Chinese girl, her hair done up in aluminum curlers, could be another manifestation of Medusa. Eugene passes up the opportunity to confront her; instead, he moves on to a condition in which actual language loses its power while other signs, like the tattoo of the butterfly, reverse or scramble all previous understandings. Patricia S. Yaeger's interpretation of *The Golden Apples,* "'Because a Fire Was in My Head': Eudora Welty and the Dialogic Imagination," brilliantly teases these reversals out of the text, disclosing the feminist strategy by which Welty "reveal[s] the limits of [Yeats's] mythology of gender while extending the imaginative power that this mythology brings to male speakers to women as well."[6] Welty's reversal of mythologies and the redistribution of naming power over experience occur most densely in "Music from Spain."

The key interpreter of these meanings, so Eugene concludes, is the Spanish guitarist whom he spots on a downtown street. Eugene and Emma had seen the guitarist perform the previous evening, but the resonance he has for Eugene goes beyond his musical performance:

> He walked across the stage without a glance at the audience—an enormous man in an abundant dress suit with long, heavy tails. As he reached the center front of the stage and turned gravely—he seemed serious as a doctor—his head looked weighty too, long and broad together, with black-rimmed glasses circling his eyes and his hair combed back to hang behind him almost to his shoulders, like an Indian, or the old senator from back home. (172)

In Eugene's imagination and memory, the guitarist knots several of the key associations of the central male figure of *The Golden Apples,* his father, King: the formal suit, the flowing hair, the prominent eyes, the association with Vardaman—"the old senator from back home."

Eugene's pursuit of the guitarist is punctuated with demolitions of the feminine. At a street corner, he and the guitarist wait next to an exotic woman birthmarked "as a butterfly is, all over her visible skin," and wearing a hat suggestive of Medusa "with curving bright feathers about her head" (174). Eugene steers the guitarist away from this danger. Just as soon, another danger appears in a sideshow with a fat lady attraction. The illustration of the fat lady makes Eugene think, with disgust, of his wife and of all women (175).

Eugene treats the Spaniard to lunch, and the man eats it greedily. Out on the street again, the pair is greeted by another token of a campaign to eradicate women:

> As they paused on the walk, a streetcar not far away roared down a crowded street. With the air of a fool or a traitor, so the crowd felt all together—there was a feeling like a concussion in the air—a dumpy little woman tripped forward on high heels in the street, swung her purse like a hatful of flowers, spilling everything and sunk in an outrageous pink color in the streetcar's path. In a moment the streetcar struck her. She was pitched about, thrown ahead on the tracks, then let alone; she was not run over by the car, but she was dead. (182–83)

As a projection of the violent end Eugene might wish for Emma, this incident is powerfully expressive.

Eugene and his guest reach the sea finally, land's end. There they are surrounded by myriad waste land images: another sideshow with a "shouting mechanical dummy of a woman" (190), "a black scraggly wood" (191), huge rats (194). The intensity of the landscape loosens Eugene's tongue and he harasses the Spaniard with a confession of his own sins: the slapping of Emma and his lack of remorse. When the Spaniard instead offers Eugene forgiveness with a mariposa lily, Eugene grasps the man and tries to toss him off the rocks into the sea.

The Spaniard resists, and the ferocity of his resistance throws Eugene off balance. The Spaniard, in turn, must save Eugene. The mutual embrace seems to Eugene the blocked ritual of physical renewal, with Emma, that he has been resisting both actively and passively for at least the year since their daughter's death. A word would unlock the jam, but Eugene cannot utter it (198). He and the Spaniard, his father surrogate, come down from the height of meaning, reenter the mundane streets, and surrender any possibility of healing speech or act.

Having coffee with Eugene's last coins, they are served by a woman who reestablishes the failure of heterosexual intimacy in marriage:

"Go to hell," she said resonantly to Eugene. "In my country I have a husband. He too is a little man, and sits up as small as you. When he is bad, I peek him up, I stand him on the mantelpiece." (200)

With this anticlimactic warning echoing, Eugene hurries back to Emma only to find her gossiping with a neighbor. They have also been discussing a Spaniard, probably the same one who has been Eugene's companion. The most they can say about him is that he suffers from indigestion—a social faux pas—and he needs a haircut (201–2). Eugene, who could perhaps enliven this chat with some news from his day, remains silent.

A cursory discussion of "Music from Spain" cannot claim to do justice to its finesse, Welty's command of language, gesture, and image. The autobiographical dimension of Eugene's travail and hope in San Francisco adds to the compactness of the story's meanings. Welty began the story while she herself was living in San Francisco in 1948, almost the same age as Eugene. Like her character, an exile from Mississippi, Welty had gone West to visit a friend, John Robinson, and to see if she could continue to write far from native ground. Eugene's pursuit of the artist can be read as the script of Welty's own pursuit of her life as a successfully working artist away from the necessary confines of home and past in Mississippi. When Eugene imagines himself in quest of the Spaniard,

> Suppose he [Eugene] was still in the process of leaving Mississippi—not stopped here, but simply an artist, touring through,

Welty is using her own experience with willed exile (178).

If "Music from Spain" explores the territory of exile, then "The Wanderers" attempts to reconcile homecoming with individual ambition and dream. "The Wanderers" brings Virgie Rainey, after years away from Morgana, back to her mother's house. She has been there some time when Katie Rainey dies and Virgie, like Laurel Hand in the later novel *The Optimist's Daughter* (1972), must settle the household and sort out the meanings of her life.

The meanings are, of course, social and cultural. "The Wanderers" is scrupulous with its depiction of the ways in which the funeral ritual must be conducted in a small southern town. There is a form to be followed, and the community will enforce it sometimes over the will and feelings of the individual bereaved. Virgie suffers kin from all over the region to descend upon her house; she endures expressions of condolence from people she does not necessarily like; she takes with stoic, female, equanimity the manipulation of her feelings by men who prove themselves worthless in the grieving process.

"The Wanderers" is the woman's story, taking the complications of the male/female friction of the earlier stories and resolving them in favor of Virgie's own apotheosis as an unpartnered woman, a woman whose fulfillment can be achieved on her own. Rebecca Mark explores this intertextual territory fully in her *The Dragon's Blood: Feminist Intertextuality in Eudora Welty's "The Golden Apples."*[7]

It is a dry September, an exhausted and water-starved nature, in which "The Wanderers" begins. Lizzie Stark survives, and looks from her windows out upon the house where Katie had held sway as her class and temperamental opposite:

> looking down over her hill, the burned, patchy grass no better than Katie Rainey's, and the thirsty shrubs; but the Morgan sweet olive, her own grandmother's age, her grandmother's tree, was blooming. (203–4)

The single source of living continuity is the woman's tree, and it introduces a system of symbols linked to female endurance in the final story.

The central symbol in the constellation is the female body itself. Katie, in the last moments of her life, feeling in her own body the mortal pain, recognizes the meaning:

> "There's nothing Virgie Rainey loves better than struggling against a real hard plaid," Miss Katie thought, with a thrust

of pain from somewhere unexpected. Whereas, there was a
simple line down through her own body now, dividing it in
half; there should be one in every woman's body—it would
need to be the long way, not the cross way—that was too
easy—making each of them a side to feel and know, and a
side to stop it, to be waited on, finally. (207)

The blow of Perseus's blade emphasizes the horizontal division
of the woman's body, slicing the head from the traditional seat
of emotions—heart and womb. This division satisfies a male
mythology of woman as the unstable compound of intellect and
urge. Mark and Yaeger have found Welty's textual resistance
to this male definition of woman. "The Wanderers," they con-
vincingly show, builds to the conclusion that women—the
woman, Virgie—exercise a particular kind of self-determination, inhabit whole bodies in which intellect and sensation are
organized into a coherent self. The "plaid" against which Virgie has been struggling since "June Recital" is the long-standing, male-authorized belief that a woman cannot be both a
thinking person and a physical object.

King, who makes a farewell appearance in "The Wanderers," having come back to an unenthusiastic Snowdie in his
dotage, is a relic of his own myth, the myth that women actually
enjoy being his prey because there is something "natural" in that
relationship which his behavior releases. The last woman in *The
Golden Apples* to believe that is the dead woman herself, Katie
Rainey.

The surviving men of Morgana, the putative heirs of King,
are a sorry lot in "The Wanderers." Mr. Nesbitt, the ogler of

"Moon Lake," comes to mourn Katie but actually spends his time trying to talk Virgie into admitting that she has actually enjoyed his company both as employee and dancing partner (211). A Mr. Mabry, whom gossip links with Virgie, pleads a runny nose and skips the funeral. King's sons are objects of pity. Eugene is dead and buried, and Ran is a politician plump with his own denial and hypocrisy.

Welty choreographs the complicated situation in order to do justice to a rather large cast of fictional characters whose individual fates call for disposition. For example, Nina Carmichael, last seen as an adolescent girl fascinated with Easter in "Moon Lake," appears at Katie's funeral as a pregnant wife. She is married to a Nesbitt, the family that is denuding the Morgana forest for lumber. The final glimpse of Nina is keyed to the evening in Easter's tent when she (Nina) felt the night personified as the forbidden yet desirable male to whom Easter's hand was outstretched in welcome. Nina's "puffed white arm stretched along the sewing machine" signifies the ennui of a blunted imagination. That she is bored and perhaps unwell is hinted by her father-in-law, the officious Mr. Nesbitt, who threatens to cheer her up (211).

Cassie Morrison returns as well, her "black-stockinged legs" consistent with formal mourning and with her self-imposed existence as a nun consecrated to the memory of her dead mother (209). Cassie's shrine to the memory of Catherine Morrison is a symbol of memory exaggerated into obsession. Cassie has spelled out her mother's name in narcissi:

"Two hundred and thirty-two bulbs! And then Miss Katie's hyacinthus all around those, and I've got it bordered in violets, you know, to tell me where it is in summer!" (239)

Her brother, Loch, has escaped to New York; he never visits. And Mr. Morrison, another male derelict, has been helpless since his wife's sudden suicide. Catherine Morrison haunts "The Wanderers" as she had flitted temptingly just beyond firm interpretation in "June Recital." Juba, a black woman who worked for Katie, has seen Mrs. Morrison's ghost:

> "I seen that Mrs. Morrison from 'cross the road in long white nightgown, no head atall, in her driveway Saddy. Rackanize her freckle arms. You ever see her? I seen her here. She die in pain?" (238)

Cassie's mother is one more female victim to the Perseid violence of life.

Before she leaves, though, Virgie bathes in the Big Black River, a ritual cleansing between stages of her mother's funeral ceremonies. The imagery in the scene is very sensual, bringing the female body to the apex of its power to encompass the world:

> She saw her waist disappear into reflectionless water; it was like walking into sky, some impurity of skies. All was one warmth, air, water, her own body. All seemed one weight, one matter—until as she put down her head and closed her eyes and the light slipped under her lids, she felt this matter a translucent one, the river, herself,

the sky all vessels which the sun filled. She began to swim in the river, forcing it gently, as she would wish for gentleness to her body. Her breasts around which she felt the water curving were as sensitive at that moment as the tips of wings must feel to birds, or antennae to insects. She felt the sand, grains intricate as little cogged wheels, minute shells of old seas, and the many dark ribbons of grass and mud touch her and leave her, like suggestions and withdrawals of some bondage that might have been dear, now dismembering and losing itself. She moved like a cloud in skies, aware but only of the nebulous edges of her feeling and vanishing opacity of her will, the carelessness for the water as for what was ahead. (219)

Virgie takes in the world, dissolved in the river, as she would wish to take a human lover. That there has been no human lover of gentleness and power anywhere near what Virgie can achieve privately is also expressed in her ecstasy. Although Virgie physically divests herself of Morgana and is poised to leave at the conclusion of the story, this moment merging with water is her spiritual departure. Water dissolves the other elements and becomes Virgie's enraptured lover, a not-self that fulfills and complements her.

That Virgie's rapture in this moment is gendered and not universally human is indicated in the accumulating associations of the sexes and water. Easter plunges into Moon Lake and seems almost to try to elude rescue by Loch. Miss Lizzie shoulders into his attempts to revive Easter with an apparent aside that resonates in the symbolic register of the text: "'You little rascal,

I bet you run down and pollute the spring, don't you?'" (130). The Spaniard whom Eugene pursues for the secret of identity and paternity commemorates their reaching the waves of "Land's End" by "[making] water toward the sea, throwing up a rampart, a regular castle, in the sand" (191). Women and water are one; men and water are nonfraternizing foes.

Virgie's imminent departure from Morgana is not only the native daughter's demonstration that the actual paraphernalia of place are not essential to identity. More widely it is the Woman's declaration that the Male (personified by King and a host of replicas) is not indispensable to her identity. Whether or not Virgie actually leaves Morgana is less important than the promise implicit in "The Wanderers." Even though cutting off Medusa's head was the "heroic act, perhaps," Virgie knew the way to transcendence was not in severing but in encompassing. Miss Eckhart had shown the way, but the way was inchoate in Virgie all along. Seeing things in their time, neither as repetitions of the past nor as prophecies of the future, kept Virgie safe from the incarceration of imitation, safe from ideological capture, the black-stockinged sentence of Cassie, the puffed-arm ennui Nina, the terminal vulgarity of Jinny Love, or the headless undead wandering of Mrs. Morrison.

CHAPTER SIX

The Ponder Heart

From the day of its publication (*The New Yorker* 1953 and Harcourt, Brace 1954), *The Ponder Heart* impressed readers and critics alike with the peculiar nature of its humor. Ranked by sheer number of reviews alone, *The Ponder Heart* was probably Welty's most immediately "embraced" book. There was scarcely a discouraging word. Louis D. Rubin Jr., reviewing for *The Baltimore Sun,* saw Welty playing Chekhov to Faulkner's Dostoyevsky. Charmed by Welty's humor, Rubin took a bead on a more serious side to the story: "the strong sense of community, of social structure. All the people in the town of Clay know each other, and know exactly where they stand."[1] Charles Poore, in the prestigious "Books of the [New York] Times" review, saw Welty as Mozart to Faulkner's Wagner or Beethoven. Picking up Porter's left-handed praise from her introduction to *A Curtain of Green,* Poore wrote that Welty was "a natural born storyteller" at the top of her art.[2] V. S. Pritchett, noting that Welty had avoided the pitfalls that usually engulf the regional writer, lauded Welty's "depth and technical skill" seasoned with "a sardonic comic brio."[3]

These examples of wide success with reviewers project the happy fate of *The Ponder Heart.* The challenge has been to explain the coexistence of the comic and the foreboding, Mozart and Wagner. Harrison Smith, at one time an editor who had declined to publish a collection of Welty's short fiction and photographs in the late 1930s, observed in his syndicated newspaper review of *The Ponder Heart* that Welty's work "could have been a depressing tragedy instead of the highly entertaining comedy it actually is."[4] Counting most contemporary writers as connoisseurs of misery, Smith was happy to find *The Ponder Heart* an exception to fashion.

The Ponder Heart is farce with an aftertaste. Four decades of criticism later, the debate is still divided between those who concentrate on the comedy and those who savor what Harrison Smith saw as the tragedy at bay. In her study of Welty's work (1986 [1962]), Ruth Vande Kieft targets the central conflict as psychological:

Lacking the wisdom of the serpent, Uncle Daniel is as foolish as a dove; lacking a trace of "common sense," he borders on insanity. Out of the clash between the foolishness of his "wisdom" and the "foolishness" of the ordinary world of selfishness and calculation, zany relationships and muddles develop.[5]

As the muddles compound, "zany" inches toward "tragedy," Vande Kieft explains. In the end, though, she does not see *The Ponder Heart* as succumbing to darkness: "But the story does not seem meant to be taken very seriously" (56).

Robert B. Holland, in one of the first critical essays on *The Ponder Heart* to appear in an academic journal, extends the theme of conflict in the story by linking it to conflict between content and form. "The eccentric and farcical behavior of the characters in *The Ponder Heart* belies the harmony of its verbal rendition as it belies the metaphysical order of the 'South-

ern design,' and as the symmetry of this design is belied by the
injustices committed in its name."[6] Echoing the point made by
Louis Rubin in his review—that the community of Clay is a
microcosm of the idealized community of the South—Holland
positions Welty's novella as part of a conservative cultural
defense of the South, embattled in the 1950s by legal and social
forces seeking to overturn segregation. Conflict, therefore,
resides in the culture represented by the form of the story:
Southerners defend themselves against "certain kinds of ugli-
ness and violence" in their "place" by communicating in forms
of "verbal symmetry" (358, 355).

Alfred Appel follows a well-worn critical path. He repeats
Holland's point—that the characters' "verbalizations" create
and maintain a "true community"—without extending it.[7] And
he concludes his brief discussion, under the heading of "The
Comic Spirit," with the statement that when what is unsaid is
mixed with the actual monologue, the result is tragic in scope
(60).

Michael Kreyling's *Eudora Welty's Achievement of Order*
(1980) gravitates to the darker side of *The Ponder Heart* and
attempts to pick out the "tragic" threads of Welty's imagination
in the comic fabric of the story. In taking that approach,
Kreyling follows the cues of Katherine Anne Porter, who, in
the famous introduction to *A Curtain of Green,* preferred to see
the narrator of "Why I Live at the P.O." (with whom Edna
Earle is often paired in critical studies of Welty's first-person
narrators) as a case study in dementia praecox rather than as a
delightful, somewhat zany postmistress struggling to maintain
her sanity when all around her are losing theirs. Up to the pre-

sent, these divisions of opinion continue to define attempts to understand Welty's comic sense. A potentially fruitful contemporary departure is Sharon Baris's exploration of *The Ponder Heart's* intimate, if surreptitious, ties to its political-social context beyond the South in the years of the Rosenberg trials and the Red Scare.

Critical consensus, then, seems to hold that the achievement of *The Ponder Heart* is its humor, and that the humor is generated by the collision of the irresistible "comic" force, Uncle Daniel Ponder, and the immovable "tragic" object, his cousin Edna Earle. Welty had used a similar collision plot before *The Ponder Heart,* and would use it later, although not to comic ends, in *The Optimist's Daughter.* In general terms the plot is this: A woman represents and in a certain sense *embodies* order and restraint, the values of an Apollonian worldview in which the promptings of the physical appetite are seen as chaotic and destructive to the attainment of community order and social continuity. In the short story "Asphodel," the character of Miss Sabina sails under this flag. Surrounded by images and figures of classical stillness, repose, and the ideal of stasis, Sabina struggles to freeze relentless forces of change often embodied in Dionysian male characters: her father and the husband, Don McInnis, he chose for her. The intention in the male/female patterning seems authorized when, at the climax of the story, Don McInnis reappears in the ruins of Asphodel as a satyr—naked and surrounded by a flock of goats.

Porter's preference for "Why I Live at the P.O." as a quasi-documentary story exploring varieties of southern small-town depravity goes, perhaps, too far in creating a dark side to

Welty's comic vision, but some darkness is clearly discernible on the outskirts of the story. Sister's nirvana is finally reached at the end of the story when she has moved out of the rambunctious family house and into her own quarters, where she can rest easy psychologically, knowing that there is a place for everything and everything is in its place. There will be no unexpected intrusions, such as a younger sister and a surprise niece, at the post office in China Grove.

The Ponder Heart, viewed as a point in the continuity of this theme in Welty's work, is lodged in the heart of her imaginative vision. The stories of *The Bride of the* Innisfallen, published in 1955, two years after *The Ponder Heart,* but written and published individually while Welty was working through Edna Earle's story, provide further confirmation. Each of these stories, keyed to the "bride" in the title story, concerns an encounter between a woman who seeks some kind of completion in a relationship with a male, and the male who has no idea or intention of playing the role of fulfilling another. The stories in *The Bride of the* Innisfallen are difficult and serious, and soured not a few reviewers. In *The Ponder Heart,* Welty treated the same subject matter with comedy that seems to have pleased everyone.

Naming her heroine Edna Earle, Welty sets the novella spinning ironically from the beginning. Edna Earle is the heroine of Augusta Jane Evans's novel *St. Elmo* (1866), the *Gone with the Wind* of the nineteenth century. Edna Earle, orphaned early in her life, aspires to become a woman of letters. She must endure the neglect of those (male and female) who cannot even begin to think of a woman in a literary career, and she must weather the lascivious attentions of St. Elmo Murray, Byronic world-traveler, heart-breaker, roué, anti-comic version of Uncle Daniel. In the end, Edna Earle achieves both success as an intellectual and writer *and* a proposal of marriage from St. Elmo—who takes holy orders when nothing else will persuade Edna Earle that he has renounced his rakish ways. By way of consenting, or perhaps capitulating, Edna Earle faints. The vexed importance of Evans's heroine in Welty's fiction—not just in *The Ponder Heart*—is explored by Peter Schmidt in his *The Heart of the Story: Eudora Welty's Short Fiction.*[8]

Welty's Edna Earle possesses a thicker skin than Evans's, but her situation, although it diverges from her predecessor's in many circumstantial ways, runs parallel in certain basic ways. Both characters, as female, are largely or wholly ignored when they act like or ask to be considered as responsible adults. Evans's heroine has to grapple for education, and even when she achieves it most of the men and women she encounters tend to think of her as an aberration unless and until she marries someone in her station and puts her intellectual light under the proper bushel.

Welty's Edna Earle has an easier time being an "intellectual." Since Uncle Daniel Ponder was his parents' youngest and last child, and Edna Earle's father was their firstborn, uncle and niece were close together in elementary school. "I did pass him in the seventh grade," Edna Earle confesses, "and hated to do it, but I was liable to have passed anybody. People told me I ought to have been the *teacher*" (5). Academic study is not the only definition of "smart" as far as Edna Earle is concerned. Like Evans's Edna Earle, Welty's is faced with providing a living for herself. There are two ways in twentieth-century Clay, Mississippi, as there had been two in the nineteenth. A woman can inherit property or marry it. Welty's Edna Earle faces a problem in both directions. Dynastically, Uncle Daniel has prior claim to the Ponder fortune as the only surviving male child of the reigning patriarch, old Sam Ponder. Edna Earle's mother "just had me [Edna Earle] and quit" and her father, presumably too rebellious to endure Sam's controlling paternal style, "left home at an early age, nobody ever makes the mistake of asking about *him*" (7). Edna Earle must find some wealth on which to stand (for the prospect of a husband in the peripatetic Mr. Springer seems a mirage), and she succeeds in getting the Beulah Hotel from Daniel by using her wits. In order to tie his son to some kind of domestic routine, Sam Ponder schemes to marry him off. Marriage to Miss Teacake Magee (Edna Earle's find), a Baptist widow, does not last long. Edna Earle, sensing her opening, "asked [Daniel] one question about [Miss Teacake] and got this hotel" (19). Cunning is the last defense of the conquered.

The more conventional means of marrying a provider proves, for Edna Earle, less satisfactory. Her only gentleman caller is an itinerant wonder-drug salesman who seems to have a more intimate relationship with his automobile and the road than he has (or wishes to have) with Edna Earle. She has entertained the possibility of marriage to Mr. Springer, the salesman, but the future seems anything but romantic:

Poor Grandpa! Suppose I'd even *attempted,* over the years, to step off—I dread to think of the lengths Grandpa would have gone to to stop it. Of course, I'm intended to look after Uncle Daniel and everybody knows it, but in plenty of marriages there's three—three all your life. Because nearly everybody's got somebody. I used to think if I ever did step off with, say, Mr. Springer, Uncle Daniel wouldn't mind; he always could make Mr. Springer laugh. And I could name the oldest child after Grandpa and win him over quick before he knew it. Grandpa adored compliments, though he tried to hide it. Ponder Springer—that sounds perfectly plausible to me, or did at one time. (18)

Edna Earle's dynastic plans are doubly thwarted. First, Mr. Springer seems unwilling and uninterested in becoming her consort. He is either out of town or too sleepy to sit up when he is in Clay. Second, Daniel always seems liable to produce an heir just when Edna Earle thinks she has him "protected."

Like his predecessors in earlier work by Welty—for example, Don McInnis in "Asphodel," Mr. Whitaker in "Why I Live at the P.O.," King MacLain in *The Golden Apples*—Daniel Ponder embodies a (male) principle of random if not randy propagation. What Edna Earle needs from Mr. Springer in order to put some dynastic cards in her hand, Daniel gives away to all and sundry. He is particularly susceptible to an erotic energy that Edna Earle, and the Apollonian women who precede her in Welty's works, are devoted to keeping in check, or out of his ken altogether. Marriage to Teacake Magee was, arguably, a strategy to decoy the erotic toward domestic control. Daniel is dangerously close to haring off after carnival performer Intrepid Elsie Fleming when Miss Teacake is flung in his path:

> Intrepid Elsie Fleming rode a motorcycle around the Wall of Death—which let her do, if she wants to ride a motorcycle that bad. It was the time she wasn't riding I objected to—when she was out front on the platform warming up her motor. That was nearly the whole time. You could hear her day and night in the remotest parts of this hotel and with the sheet over your head, clear over the sound of the Merry-Go-Round and all. She dressed up in pants. (15)

As much as Edna Earle wants to blot out the siren call, she fails. Daniel can hear it in spite of her interference.

The siren shows up in the particular person of Bonnie Dee Peacock: simultaneously a farce of mature female sexuality and an exposé of the manipulative desires of a male-controlled sexual market. One of the facets of the "dark" side of *The Ponder Heart* is the extent to which it buys into a popular style of the doll-like female:

> I wish you could have seen Bonnie Dee! I wish you could. I guess I'd known she was living, but I'd never given her a real good look. She was just now getting her breath. Baby yellow hair, downy—like one of those dandelion puff-balls you can blow and tell the time by. And not a grain beneath. Now Uncle Daniel may not have a whole *lot* of brains, but what's there is Ponder, and no

mistake about it. But poor little old Bonnie Dee! There's
a world of difference. He talked and she just stood there
and took her fill of my rummage sale, held up there under
the tree, without offering a word. She was little and she
was dainty, under the dust of that trip. But I could tell by
her little coon eyes, she was shallow as they come. (24)

Reinforcing the image of Bonnie Dee as a baby doll in a
sideshow of male desire, her debut in the story is heralded by
images of buying and selling. Edna Earle remarks that Bonnie
Dee's only expertise seems to be clerking in the Clay dime
store. And Edna Earle herself first lays eyes on her future aunt
while she (Edna Earle) is running a rummage sale for the sup-
posed benefit of Christian missions to the "colored" races—
"two dollars and ninety-five cents to the good of the heathen,
selling away to the Negroes as hard as I could" (21). Selling to
Negroes for the benefit of missions to peoples of color in far-
flung parts of the globe opens a window of irony on this idealized southern community, and suggests that Welty was not on
the sidelines in the political debates of the day.

If Edna Earle's participation in a racially oppressive society in Clay, Mississippi, while doing good works for the missions is risky critical ground, her fear and jealousy of Bonnie
Dee is not. Most of her overt resistance to Bonnie Dee as
Daniel's wife has to do with the Peacocks's social standing.
They are "the kind of people keep the mirror outside on the
front porch, and go out and pick railroad lilies to bring inside
the house, and wave at trains till the day they die" (20). Edna
Earle's covert suspicion and fear flow from a feminist/Apol-

lonian reservoir. Working in a dime store is not the only thing
Bonnie Dee is good for; sex may be another. The power of
erotic self-determination—Elsie Fleming warming up her
motor at all hours—is the one kind of freedom Edna Earle
wishes to control under the contorted cover of Christian charity and domestic omnicompetence:

> Well, as I opened the subject by saying when I sat down,
> I can't *help* being smarter than Uncle Daniel. I don't even
> try, myself, to make people happy the way they should
> be; they're so stubborn. I just try to give them what they
> think they want. (41)

What Daniel thinks he wants is Elsie Fleming or the chorines at
the fair—or Bonnie Dee. But Edna Earle conspires to keep Elsie
and the dancers away from Daniel, and she tries to keep the married couple apart when they split by supplying Bonnie Dee with
cash so that the estranged wife will not have to face Daniel.

The love that Edna Earle prefers is less physical and individualized than it is communal. Critics and reviewers who spot-
ted this theme in *The Ponder Heart* were not mistaken. When
Uncle Daniel modifies his generalized largesse and communal
love and targets desire on Bonnie Dee (after a few preliminary
misses), Edna Earle's protective instincts swing into action. She
explains herself under the banner of love rather than desire:

> I don't know if you can measure love at all. But Lord
> knows there's a lot of it, and seems to me from all the
> studying I've done over Uncle Daniel—and he loves

more people than you and I put together ever will—that
if the main one you've set your heart on isn't speaking
for your love, or is out of your reach some way, married
or dead, or plain nitwitted, you've still got that love
banked up somewhere. What Uncle Daniel did was just
bestow his all around quick—men, women, and children.
Love! There's always somebody wants it. Uncle Daniel
knew that. He's smart in a way you aren't, child. (50–51)

Edna Earle's wisdom comes from deprivation. Mr. Springer,
the individualized target of her love, does not reciprocate. If he
takes her to a movie, it is usually "one of those sad Monday
night movies and [he] never holds my hand in the right places"
(54). Hopes of continuing the Ponder name are rapidly fading.
The visit to Polk for the burial of Bonnie Dee throws in Edna
Earle's face the fact that in spite of low social class the Peacocks have plenty of each other. When they all gather in Clay
for the trial of Uncle Daniel, Edna Earle realizes again:
"*They're* not dying out" (63).

The trial of Uncle Daniel for the wrongful death of Bonnie
Dee Peacock brings some of these thematic issues to a head by
way of the stock machinery of the courtroom drama. Ostensi-
bly it is the wish of Edna Earle and DeYancey Clanahan,
Daniel's defense attorney, that the accused *not* take the stand
on the grounds that he has nothing to explain and would jeop-
ardize his own case by allowing the prosecution to cross-exam-
ine him. After all, an innocent so full of love could not possibly
have wished or effected such harm. Edna Earle is more active
than Daniel's lawyer in this strategy, maintaining after her tes-

timony (later proved to be perjured) that "I'm the go-between, that's what I am, between my family and the world. I hardly ever get a word in for myself" (89). This disclaimer is patently untrue: *The Ponder Heart* is Edna Earle's monologue and no one but she herself gets a word in any of it.

More significant, however, is the story Edna Earle attempts to block by telling her perjured one. Dorris Gladney, a vaudeville exaggeration of a prosecuting attorney, prefers a lurid version he tries to elicit from each of the state's witnesses. Finishing with Narciss, the black woman who cooks for the Ponders in the country, Gladney strikes home with his version in the bold letters of a tabloid front page:

> "Mr. Daniel Ponder, like Othello of old, Narciss, he entered yonder and went to his lady's couch and he suffocated to death that beautiful, young, innocent, ninety-eight-pound bride of his, out of a fit of pure-D jealousy from the well-springs of his aging heart." (72)

Such is not the kind of love—jealous, retributive, paranoid—that Edna Earle wants identified with "the Ponder heart." She concocts a cover story in which a ball of fire triggered by an opportune thunderstorm scares Bonnie Dee to death before either she or Daniel can get to her. Lying to protect the Ponder heart does not strike Daniel well. When Edna Earle resumes her seat next to him in court, "he looked at me like he never saw me before in his life" (89).

It is not just that Edna Earle's version of events is untrue, although perjury is bad enough and undermines her earlier claims to be the moral backbone of the Clay community. The version of events that Daniel tells—presumably the "true" version—discloses aspects of lived experience that Edna Earle would rather keep off the record. In Daniel's version, Bonnie Dee is alive but frightened when he and Edna Earle join her in the Ponder living room during a fierce electrical storm. Being afraid of lightning, Bonnie Dee tries to hide by burrowing into the cushions of a sofa. When Uncle Daniel tries to calm her fears by tickling her, he only quickens her suffocation (104). In a sense he is "guilty" of manslaughter. It is not, however, the legal verdict of the court that so much troubles Edna Earle as it is a revelation of the sexual component to Daniel's relationship with Bonnie Dee.

The detail with which Welty fills Daniel's testimony seems strong enough to support some speculation on this subtext:

She [Bonnie Dee] pulled herself in a little knot at the other end of the sofa [from Daniel]. Here came a flash of lightning bigger than the rest, and thunder on top of it, and she buried her face in the pillow and started to cry. So the tassel of Grandma's antimacassar came off in Uncle Daniel's hand and he reached out and tickled her with it, on the ankle.

The storm got closer and he tickled a little more. He made the little tassel travel up to her knee. He wouldn't call it touching her—it was tickling her; though she didn't want one any more right now than the other. . . .

And all the while it was more like a furnace in there, and noisy and bright as Kingdom Come. Grandpa Pon-

der's house shook! And Bonnie Dee rammed harder into
the pillow and shrieked and put out her hands behind her,
but that didn't do any good. When the storm got right
over the house, he went right to the top with "creep-
mousie," up between those bony little shoulder blades to
the nape of her neck and her ear—with the sweetest, most
forbearing smile on his face, a forgetful smile. Like he
forgot everything then that she ever did to him, how
changeable she'd been. . . .

Her hands fluttered and stopped, then her whole little
length slipped out from under his fingers, and rolled
down to the floor, just as easy as nod, and stayed there—
with her dress up to her knees and her hair down over her
face. (103–4)

What Edna Earle has narrated, and had been forced to watch as
if from ringside in the room itself, is the intimate history of
Daniel and Bonnie Dee which she has striven to keep out of the
story of the Ponder heart by steering the possibilities of the word
"love" into the communal and definitely away from the erotic. In
Welty's other stories where this pattern of character, imagery,
and narrative also exists, that which is denied voice always ultimately gets to "speak." In "Asphodel" Don McInnis disrupts the
shapely narration of the three ladies who ritually remember
Sabina. In *The Golden Apples*—in "June Recital" particularly—
the muted subtext of sexual aggression and response speaks up
when, at the conclusion of that story, Jinny Love Stark swears,
ultimately vainly, that she and all her cohort will remain old
maids. Her oath is triggered by the sight of naked Loch Morrison

and his "little, tickling thing." Uncle Daniel's tickling echoes Loch's, underlining in the scene(s) of Bonnie Dee's death the latent presence of unfulfilled sexual desire.

Broadway, understandably, made nothing of the subtext to *The Ponder Heart.* It was adapted for the stage by Joseph Fields and Jerome Chodorov and had a respectable run early in 1956. The Fields and Chodorov version exploits the broad comedy of *The Ponder Heart,* expanding on already broad stereotypes such as Narciss, the Peacocks, and Dorris Gladney. When the reviewers and critics first encountered *The Ponder Heart* and mapped out what have proven to be reliable coordinates to its accomplishment (the theme of community and the nature of Welty's comedy as propelled by undisclosed "tragic" sources), they were responding to the printed text. If the stage version lifts the broad strokes of character to the level of cliché, literary-critical readings of the text move more deeply into the tangled human condition from which Welty's kind of storytelling evolves.

CHAPTER SEVEN

The Bride of the Innisfallen

If, in the general trends of views and reviews of Eudora Welty's works, one book sparks the most controversy, it is (and will continue to be) *The Bride of the* Innisfallen *and Other Stories* (1955). Accustomed to what they considered "southern" stories of humor, local color, eccentric characters, image patterns from classical mythology or Anglo-Celtic folklore, book reviewers were surprised when these seven stories were brought out by Harcourt, Brace right after *The Ponder Heart.* John K. Hutchens, reviewing for the *New York Herald Tribune Books,* crept up to his comments on "Miss Welty's Somewhat Puzzling Art" by reminding his readers that just prior to *The Bride of the* Innisfallen, Welty had written "*The Ponder Heart,* swift, straightforward, witty, warm and alive with a sense of a storyteller's pleasure in telling a story." These new stories, Hutchens fretted, were "intense, inward-looking, elaborately unplotted" and might even have come from the hands of Porter, Woolf, or Bowen.[1] Sterling North's curmudgeonly syndicated review cracked wise: the hypothetical new critical book on Welty should be titled *The Mixed Metaphors of Miasmic Fiction: Or, the Wandering Weltschmerz of Eudora Welty.* North recognized "labored but noteworthy effects," but only when Welty dealt with "the region she knows best—the deep South."[2] Even staunch defender William Peden, who granted Welty the status of "virtuoso," was hard-pressed to like the stories in *The Bride.* He confessed he found them "in some ways a disappointment" and "top-heavy, overburdened by mass of detail and obscure or indecipherable symbol."[3] The reviews of *The Bride,* taken in limited context, seem to indicate a sudden and abrupt shift away from native material; actually, Welty had been turning in the course of her career for several years before 1955. Three of *The Bride* stories had appeared earlier in the 1950s in *The New Yorker* and two in *Harper's Bazaar.* It was not as if the collection had appeared by stealth.

Most early critics (academics writing in scholarly and literary journals) of Welty's third collection of short stories (fourth, if you count *The Golden Apples* as short stories) read these seven stories, resistant to or largely unaware of the sexual theme and imagery which had relegated the southern local color to the background. After the first line of reviewers had complained of Welty's alleged stretching of her evocative and associational technique, there was the predictable reaction. Ruth Vande Kieft's title to her chapter on *The Bride* in *Eudora Welty* indicates a critical method and vision to assimilate the new stories to established theme and subject matter: "*The Bride of the* Innisfallen*:* From Innocence to Experience." What reviewers might have seen as overreaching is, Vande Kieft argues, consistent with Welty's previous achievement—if we keep her entire work in view. Invocation of the familiar theme of "innocence to experience" indicates a nongendered approach to the stories that more contemporary critics have shown to be limited. Vande Kieft further shows her literary-critical approach in her thesis sentence to the chapter, a sentence unchanged in the revised edition:

Experiment, range, and variety are apparent in the stories, but the consistency of Miss Welty's vision is equally apparent in her continued focus on love and separateness, the human mysteries, the sense of exposure and need for protection, the comprehension of human experience through rare moments of genuine communication with another, or through private, unshared insight.[4]

Borrowing Robert Penn Warren's durable insight into Welty's theme of "love and separateness" and adding the theme of the tension between individual self-consciousness and the needs of community, Vande Kieft locates *The Bride of the* Innisfallen in a Welty oeuvre and links the whole to established traditions of literary interpretation.

Alfred Appel Jr., whose study of Welty, *A Season of Dreams* (1965), concludes with a chapter on *The Bride,* seems to have concurred in the mildly negative appraisals of reviewers who had found the stories obscure:

The elliptical and inconclusive form of several of the stories in this volume bears witness to her [Welty's] considerable admiration for Elizabeth Bowen. . . . The stories have less plot than ever before and it is often difficult to tell what "happens" in a given story. . . . *The Bride of the* Innisfallen is thus characterized by an acute, impressionistic rendering of the visible world; the book is appropriately dedicated to Miss Bowen.[5]

Not even a semi-favorable comparison of Welty's "impressionistic" technique to that of Monet (254) quite reconciles Appel to the fiction. There lingers in the word "acute" the hint that he thinks the work afflicted with something he cannot quite diagnose.

Michael Kreyling's work on *The Bride* attempts to heal the schism between theme and technique by arguing that critical attention should be focused on the "how" of the stories not the "what."[6] Noel Polk's "Water, Wanderers, and Weddings: Love in Eudora Welty" (1979) finds continuity in theme and imagery issuing from Welty's earlier work, particularly *Delta Wedding,* to *The Bride.* Polk has refined this approach in "Going to Naples and Other Places in Eudora Welty's Fiction."[7] These attempts at interpretation might be as far as late New Critical practice can take us. New departures through feminist and feminist/psychoanalytic criticism have revealed *The Bride* to be one of the richest works in the twentieth-century canon of women's literature. Essays by Dawn Trouard and Ruth Weston's chapter on *The Bride* in her *Gothic Traditions and Narrative Techniques in the Fiction of Eudora Welty* (1994) open new provinces of nuance and full-blown meaning we have barely approached with the older critical tools and methods.[8] Any attempt to understand the Eudora Welty of *The Bride of the* Innisfallen must be sufficiently wide in scope to take in the history of reception from review to newer theoretical and methodological approaches.

"Circe" is the oldest of the stories in *The Bride;* it was published as "Put Me in the Sky!" in the autumn 1949 issue of *Accent* and seriously revised for the collection six years later. "Circe" is a retelling of the myth in which Odysseus, on his way back to Ithaca, where Penelope faithfully waits, visits Circe's island, where his crew is transformed into a herd of swine. Welty improvises on the original myth by having

Odysseus and Circe become lovers. The heroic wanderer, hastening with all deliberate speed to Penelope, leaves Circe, the homebound nurturer, pregnant: the story ends with her queasy with morning sickness as her lover sails away. Since there is a preexisting story to which Welty's version is accountable, there is little suspense in "Circe." Welty's story stakes its claim to attention upon her ability to make the flat, two-dimensional characters of Odysseus and Circe viable as contemporary hearts and minds. Welty does this by elaborating the inner character of Circe as the willing but abandoned third side of a passionate triangle, and by flattening the heroic character of Odysseus into a love-'em-and-leave-'em cad. Welty's Odysseus is a rather muscle-bound adolescent (Loch Morrison on the wine-dark sea instead of Moon Lake) oblivious to his own narcissism and acting as if all women were fodder for his sexual grazing habits. The complementary constructions of male and female in this sexual ecology fit both *The Golden Apples* (many critics prefer to see "Circe" as the last of that phase of Welty's work) and *The Bride.*

Circe is as rich a presence as any character in *The Golden Apples.* Fiercely attached to her place, yet simultaneously hungry for another when he lands on her shores, Welty's Circe is both theme and character. All of Circe's longing, desire, and the ferocity of her sense of self in the here-and-now register in each of her actions, and in her reactions to the obliviousness of Odysseus and his men. After she serves to Odysseus's crew the broth that transforms them into swine, she and Odysseus collide. Turning her desire upon him, she bathes Odysseus and rubs his body with oil. Then she takes charge of the seduction:

> I took the chain from my waist, it slipped shining to the
> floor between us, where it lay as if it slept, as I came
> forth. Under my palms he stood warm and dense as a
> myrtle grove at noon. His limbs were heavy, braced like
> a sleep-walker's who has wandered, alas, to cliffs above
> the sea. When I passed before him, his arm lifted and
> barred my way. When I held up the glass he opened his
> mouth. He fell among the pillows, his still-open eyes two
> clouds stopped over the sun, and I lifted and kissed his
> hand. (104)

Circe desires reciprocal passion, a passion to bring her self into
being. But Odysseus fails, like all of the men in *The Bride,* by
being wrapped up in himself. The male's desire is for taking, not
for giving. His farewell kiss is mundane: "He gave me a peck-
ing, recapitulating kiss, his black beard thrust at me like a shoe.
I kissed it, his mouth, his wrist, his shoulder, I put my eyes to
his eyes, through which I saw seas toss, and to the cabinet of his
chest" (108). If Odysseus remains a locked cabinet to Circe, it
is not because he has no love to give but rather because woman
is not his primary target. His love is reserved for a dead crew-
man, the youngest, who had fallen to his death from Circe's
roof: "He [Odysseus] knelt and touched Elpenor, and like a
lover lifted him; then each in turn held the transformed boy in
his arms" (110). What there is of love and tenderness in
Odysseus is reserved for rituals of male friendship. Circe is
abandoned, full of sickness from the child in her womb, as
Odysseus and his crew flee her and the island of her passion
(107). There has been passion on Circe's island, and it has

involved the sexes, but it has not been between the sexes. "Circe" functions like an overture to *The Bride of the* Innisfallen by introducing the theme of mismatched and misdirected passion.

The formal stateliness of "Circe" aside, it is a story threading the theme of love and separateness through classical myth. That insight indeed links the story to Welty's master theme as Warren saw it in *The Wide Net,* and further corroborates her own statements that classical myths have been formative in her literary imagination from her childhood years. But more needs to be said. Love and separateness in "Circe" engages sexuality too; the bodies inflicting and suffering love and separateness are male and female bodies. As Welty retells the ancient tale, she suggests that the conventional romantic plot of complementarity in male and female may be outdated. Odysseus reserves his acts of love for homosocial ritual—bonding with his crew in mourning Elpenor. "Circe" threads the needle of "love and separateness" with greater definition than generic terms permit. Most of the stories in *The Bride of the* Innisfallen extend this opening gambit.

"The Burning," the second story in *The Bride* in order of publication, seems to be the exception. "The Burning" is Welty's sole Civil War story and one of the few she wrote that claims the "history" of the South as subject matter. For a southern writer, Welty seems distinctly unhaunted by one of the chief ghosts of the region: The Past. In fact, "The Burning" establishes its connection with the history of the South fundamentally through parody of Faulknerian style. The content and style of *Absalom, Absalom!*, *The Unvanquished,* and *Intruder in the Dust* tend to fill up the available possibilities for the southern writer dealing with Civil War history. "The Burning" slyly co-opts Faulknerian dominance.

The story concerns the burning of Jackson, Mississippi, and vicinity by William Tecumseh Sherman, who torched Atlanta in 1864 as the first move in his fiery endgame to the Civil War. The year of "The Burning," though, is 1863. Sherman was supporting Grant's siege of Vicksburg when he marauded through central Mississippi. Most of these historical names and dates are unmentioned in Welty's story; although "The Burning" is connected to historical event, it does not claim to be a version of history.

Two white sisters, Miss Theo and Miss Myra, have been left with a plantation to defend; the men of the family are either dead or off at war. The sisters have the help of one slave, Delilah, who has not yet taken the road to emancipation. Theo is the stronger sister. She looks to the here-and-now, has a sense of the dangers presented by invading Federal troops, and attempts to keep the household running on the prewar footing of racial and class hierarchy. Myra is a damaged magnolia. Locked in the past and in a fossilized role of lady as ornament, Myra is a burden to her more practical sister. Delilah is suspended between her urge to flee to freedom and a kind of mesmerized habit of obeying the white sisters.

A band of Federal troops, probably stragglers, descends upon the plantation. The scavengers proceed to loot the sisters' home of anything of value and rape each of the sisters in turn. When they have taken all they can carry, the soldiers set fire to the house. It burns to the ground. Myra, dazed in the ruins, believes—perhaps in a hallucination—that her baby is alive in the ashes, a baby who is either the offspring of an incestuous relationship with her deceased and dipsomaniac brother, or the illegitimate child of that brother and Delilah. Theo tries to slap her sister out of her fugue, but without success. The sisters seem to set out to flee the ruins, but only go far enough to find a tree from which to hang themselves. Theo, practical to the end, hangs her demented sister first. Delilah, in her first act of disobedience, declines to follow them in death. Instead she sets out on her own groping pursuit of freedom.

"The Burning" is saturated with the gothic elements of a certain type of southern historical tale. Welty's language in "The Burning" is also palpably Faulknerian at his most "rococo":

> The sisters showed no surprise to see soldiers and Negroes alike (old Ophelia in the way, talking, talking) strike into and out of the doors of the house, the front now the same as the back, to carry off beds, tables, candlesticks, washstands, cedar buckets, china pitchers, with their backs bent double; or the horses ready to go; of the food of the kitchen bolted down—and so much of it thrown away, this must be a second dinner; or the unsilenceable dogs, the old pack mixed with the strangers and fighting with all their hearts over bones. (34)

Welty shows that she can match the famous Faulknerian sentence loop for loop: rhythmic, compounded, spurred by gerundives and participles, studded here and there with the against-the-grain adjective that simultaneously expresses a quality and its opposite ("unsilenceable" for "growling" or "barking").

Tentative strands of theme link "The Burning" to the other stories in *The Bride,* but they do so darkly. Relations between male and female, for example, are limited to rape and incest. Circe's island has been invaded, and her own body despoiled, but her passion survives. Nothing of Theo and Myra survives the corresponding visitation by the predatory wanderers.

The core of *The Bride of the* Innisfallen comprises three stories published in *The New Yorker* between December 1951 and November 1952: "The Bride of the *Innisfallen*" (1 December 1951), "No Place for You, My Love" (20 September 1952), and "Kin" (15 November 1952). "The Bride of the *Innisfallen*" was, in fact, the first of Welty's stories to succeed with *The New Yorker.* It was a regular joke between Welty and Diarmuid Russell, her literary agent, that the editor of *The New Yorker,* Harold Ross, was far too blunt when it came to judging fiction, ever to appreciate Welty's work. William Maxwell, fiction editor under Ross, was Welty's champion.

"The Bride of the *Innisfallen,*" largely written at Elizabeth Bowen's home in Ireland while Welty was a guest, gives its title to the volume. Bowen had known of and admired Welty's work since *Delta Wedding,* and wrote laudatory reviews of Welty's books when they were published in England. On a renewal (1949–50) of an earlier Guggenheim Fellowship for writing and travel, Welty met Bowen in London and accepted her invitation to visit her family home in Ireland, Bowen's Court. It was there, in perhaps as rich a literary atmosphere as she had ever experienced, that Welty worked on "The Bride of the *Innisfallen*." Bowen's friendship and professional praise, the immediate Celtic surround Welty had for long admired in the work of Yeats, and the traditions represented in Russell and his father, the Irish poet and painter A. E., combined to make her stay in Ireland as intensely creative as any in her life. Edwin Weeks, the editor of *Atlantic Monthly* who had published several of her earlier stories, also on vacation in the neighborhood, could be seen fishing in the river that ran through Bowen's estate.

The title story, immediately striking many first-round readers as a study in impressionistic tones rather than plotted events, makes structural use of the ship-of-fools symbolic voyage motif to carry the main character from, as Ruth Vande Kieft succinctly put it nearly four decades ago, innocence to experience.[9] The questions are: Which of the characters on the train to the *Innisfallen,* the boat from the west coast of England to Cork, is the central character? What is the particular nature of innocence/experience in this journey?

"The American wife," not otherwise named or identified in the story, boards a train for the west of England, there to meet a boat bound for Cork. She is leaving without prior warning to her husband. Her fellow passengers, as is the pattern in such a symbolic journey, each and all reinforce the internal tension the wife feels by representing the obstacles on her course. A woman in a striped raincoat is handed into the carriage by a man, perhaps her husband, perhaps not. Is infidelity a way from innocence to experience? A young woman and a boy rush in late; she is "showing pregnancy" (50). Should innocence be preserved, as this Madonna figure surely preserves hers, in the journey from innocence to experience? A pair of lovers slip into the carriage at the last minute. Is innocence the carrot, experience the stick for life and hopes? A single man from Connemara completes the cast. Is simple withholding a way to preserve innocence?

As the train rolls out of London, the occupants of the compartment see an English child with an Irish nurse pass down the corridor. The young pregnant woman cannot contain herself:

> "Oh, isn't he *beautiful!*" the young wife cried reproachfully through the door. She would have put out her hands. (53)

Someone idly suggests that the nurse might be kidnaping the child, and the idea of danger to the mother-child relationship strikes exaggerated fear in the heart of the young wife. She responds with an acutely thematic proclamation: "'But this is *our* train,' said the young wife. 'Women alone, sometimes exceptions, but often on the long journey alone or with children'" (54). Thus the system of reference for image and incident, innocence and experience, is set. When a pair of greyhounds, sans owners, gallop into the compartment and out again, their meaning is literary rather than literal: pairedness. When a ghost story is told, the ghosts are "a pair, himself and herself" (63).

The American wife impulsively attempts to flee a similar condition, the pairedness that passion seems (in the case of Circe) to require, but which seems to her as wounding as the condition of Lord and Lady Beagle, the ghost couple (she is mad and he has a dagger stuck in him [63]). She must survive all of the talk and all of the literary signs that amount to a summons for her to return to a relationship increasingly inessential to her identity. She pushes on with the train, then with the boat to Cork.

When the boat, in a glistening dawn, enters Cork harbor, an apotheosis of the bride appears, as if aimed solely at the fleeing wife:

"There's a bride on board!" called somebody. "Look at her, look!"

Sure enough, a girl who had not yet showed herself in public now appeared by the rail in a white spring hat and, over her hands, a little old-fashioned white bunny muff. She stood there all ready to be met, now come out in her own sweet time. Delight gathered all around, singing began on board, bells could by now be heard ringing urgently in the town. Surely that color beating in their eyes came from flags hung out up the looming shore. The bride smiled but did not look up; she was looking down at her dazzling little fur muff. (79)

Sexual, religious, social, archetypal vibrations are set off by the appearance of this figure. All the strands of potential meaning must be run through the clearinghouse of the fleeing wife; it is in respect to her rejection of the massed pressure of female identity summed up in the bride apparition that the apparition has meaning.

If the story were to end at this point, the archetypal bride would carry the day: the wife should return to the cultural sanctuary symbolized in the bride. Questions about the respective natures of innocence and experience would be answered in terms of a traditionally familiar icon. But Welty sends the story on. The fleeing wife turns from the apparition of the bride and walks into the city, symbolically accepting the flux of event rather than the stasis of archetype. Ultimately she finds a telegraph office, begins to send a message to her husband ("England was a mistake.") but crumples the paper. A narrative voice pulls back from the events and muses on meanings:

> Love with the joy being drawn out of it like anything else that aches—that was loneliness; not this. *I* was nearly destroyed, she thought, and again was threatened with a light head, a rush of laughter, as when the Welshman had come so far with them and then let them off.
>
> If she could never tell her husband her secret, perhaps she would never tell it at all. You must never betray pure joy—the kind you were born and began with—either by hiding it or by parading it in front of people's eyes; they didn't want to be shown it. And still you must tell it. Is there no way? she thought—for here I am, this far. (81–82)

The fugitive wife's "pure joy" comes in a quick series of cryptic messages from surroundings: a cigarette butt tossed from a window, the window itself abstracted to a pattern of dark and light, finally a warm pub full of bodies and voices—all alien to "the girl." But she enters, finding the strangers "lovely."

If "The Bride of the *Innisfallen*" is patterned by alternating pairs and singles, that pattern must not be interpreted without the gendering that necessarily accompanies it. These are embodied pairs and singles. When the American woman turns from the bride icon, she turns as well from a surround of symbols to one of concrete sensation, from innocence as the vacating of self to experience as the only possibility for self.

"No Place for You, My Love" and "Kin," which followed "The Bride of the *Innisfallen*" in *The New Yorker* late in 1952, strengthen this suggestion. "No Place for You, My Love" has been the topic of much critical discussion; Welty herself has written an essay explaining, from the author's point of view, how she wrote the story. In her essay, Welty first holds out for the autonomy of the individual story, then relaxes that hold:

> Each story, it seems to me, thrives in the course of being written only as long as it seems to have a life of its own.
>
> Yet it may become clear to a writer in retrospect (or so it did to me, although I may have been simply tardy to see it) that his stories have repeated themselves in shadowy ways, that they have returned and may return in future too—in variations—to certain themes. They may be following, in their own development, some pattern that's been very early laid down.[10]

Welty's point is tantalizing: "very early" in what process? The author's life? The writing of this particular story? The pattern with variations set down in "No Place for You, My Love" is related to the one in "Circe," "The Bride of the *Innisfallen*," and the other stories in the collection: an ebb and flow in male/female relationship.

In what ways, though, is this pattern "shadowed"? Women are drawn to men, and vice versa, then retreat, either by choice or by necessity. In "No Place" the unnamed male who spies upon the woman in the French Quarter restaurant—a wife on holiday alone, from Ohio and therefore "at risk" in New Orleans—acts the pattern of predator, drawing a bead on his prey from the camouflage of their mutual anonymity. He finally springs her from cover when she consents to a car trip down into the wetlands south of New Orleans.

Welty repeatedly describes the marshy land as "jungle," confirming hints in the text that the man is a kind of predator who makes away with his catch. Their first stop is a ferry taking them across the Mississippi River, and when the woman has a moment to concentrate on the man in charge of the expedition into the heart of darkness, her reaction confirms his threat: "His hair in the wind looked unreasonably long and rippling. Little did he know that from here it had a red undergleam like an animal's" (10).

The feral subtext of the story is reinforced by the inclusion of an alligator on a lead, held by two boys who board the ferry. The boys laughingly ask for contestants to "rassle" their gator, but there are no takers. The gator propels the pattern running below the level of events:

> What was there so hilarious about jaws that could bite? And what danger was there once in this repulsiveness— so that the last worldly evidence of some old heroic hor-

ror of the dragon had to be paraded in capture before the
eyes of country clowns? (11)

If this is the woman's musing, then she is a skeptical Androm-
eda who feels no need of a Perseus to rescue her, since it is the
dragon who is chained and not she. If it is the man's interior
monologue, it suggests a more nuanced reaction: a vestigial
desire to act the heroic part, a sense of that part's anachronism,
a projection of his own confusion and discontent upon the
"country clowns" who serve as audience. Perhaps the coiled
control of the man at this three-sided moment communicates
itself to the woman as a species of warning, for she prays to no
deity in particular, "Deliver us all from the naked in heart" (12)
and registers anxiety just a few moments later:

Her eyes overcome with brightness and size [the "vast
open" glaring marshland], she felt a panic rise, as sudden
as nausea. Just how far below questions and answers,
concealment and revelation, they were running now—
that was still a new question, with a power of its own,
waiting. How dear—how costly—could this ride be? (13)

All of the stories in *The Bride of the* Innisfallen take their key
from this passage, for each one runs in concealment and revelation, giving away some meaning and holding back much
more. In "No Place for You, My Love," what is given the
reader is the meaning lodged in "place," the heavily seasoned
atmosphere of the Mississippi River delta south of New
Orleans: gumbo, Cajun patois, honky-tonk, the glaring light

that dissolves earth and sky in thick, moist vapor. What is held back is the meaning in the relationship, so strong and insistent that it can be personified, that seeks to swallow the couple in a hunger that is both spiritual and sexual.

When the road runs to a dead end in swamp, the two travelers stop at a honky-tonk for some food and rest. As strangers, they immediately become the targets of attention. The woman feels the strangers' eyes more acutely than the man. Like the fugitive wife in "The Bride of the *Innisfallen*," she finds the strangers' attention "lovely," even erotic:

> She lifted her head to watch him leave her, and was looked at, from all over the room. As a minute passed, no cards were laid down. In a far-off way, like accepting the light from Arcturus, she accepted it that she was more beautiful perhaps more fragile than the women they saw every day of their lives. It was just this thought coming to a woman's face, and at this hour, that seemed familiar to them. (19)

Later she and the man dance:

> He got down from his stool, and, patiently, reversing her hand in his own—just as she had had the look of being about to give up, faint—began moving her, leading her. They were dancing. . . . If they had ever been going to overstep themselves, it would be now as he held her closer and turned her, when she became aware that he could not help but see the bruise at her temple. (21–22)

Everything seems right: physical intimacy and strangeness, the bruise as indication that the woman has no need to feel loyal to the husband who inflicted it, a man set up like Odysseus in "Circe" to be masterful in his heartlessness.

But there is no permanence in consummation in "No Place for You, My Love," as there was none in "Circe" nor in "The Bride of the *Innisfallen.*" After leaving the honky-tonk, Baba's Place, the couple take a return road Dante-esque in its imagery of lakes of dust and smudge fires (24). In the waste land, these two test the doomed possibility of sex:

> At length, he stopped the car again, and this time he put his arm under her shoulder and kissed her—not knowing ever whether gently or harshly. It was the loss of that distinction that told him this was now. Then their faces touched unkissing, unmoving, dark, for a length of time. The heat came inside the car and wrapped them still, and the mosquitoes had begun to coat their arms and even their eyelids.
> Later. . . . (24–25)

The long denouement of the story legitimates the title. So close to a kind of breakthrough, the couple falls back into postcoital separateness. The sexes form an ecology in which one identity (the woman's) is the endangered species. Their separate personal sufferings prove more tolerable than the risk of something outside the lines. Like Circe and Odysseus before them, these "lovers" part.

"No Place for You, My Love" is dark in its "shadows" but "full-bodied" in its engagement with manifest and latent subject matter. As Welty writes in "Writing and Analyzing a Story":

> Of course, such a pattern [from story to story] is subjective in nature; it may lie too deep to be consciously recognized until a cycle of stories and the actions of time have raised it to view. All the same, it is a pattern of which a new story is not another copy but a fresh attempt made in its own full-bodied right and out of its own impulse, with its own pressure, and its own needs of fulfillment. (108)

The pattern that rises to the surface in "No Place for You, My Love" becomes in its turn one of the "actions of time" that raise similar patterns in "Circe," "The Bride of the *Innisfallen,*" and the other stories of this collection. This atemporal reciprocity, one story echoing in another regardless of chronology of actual composition, is the quality that distinguishes Welty's story collections, the epitome of which is *The Golden Apples,* from mere grab bags or miscellanies.

"Kin" is strongly enhanced by the gravitational field of the earlier stories too, for there are recesses in its plot that are brought to light by them. Drawing on the residue of the material Welty imaginatively assembled for *Delta Wedding,* "Kin" explores a situation in which a young woman, Dicey, engaged to become a bride, encounters the thickness of the social condition into which she is headed. A long, gossipy conversation with her aunt and cousin dredges up new and familiar lore of the "kin":

> Aunt Ethel looked patiently upwards as if she read now
> from the roof of the tester, and said, "Well, she's a
> remote cousin of Uncle Felix's, to begin with. Your third
> cousin twice removed, and your Great-aunt Beck's half-
> sister, my third cousin once removed and my aunt's half-
> sister, Dicey's—"
>
> "Don't tell me!" I cried. "I'm not that anxious to claim
> kin!" (116)

The irony of the story is, of course, that kin claims Dicey. A visit
to the Uncle Felix named in the convoluted genealogy by Aunt
Ethel unearths an old story. Felix, far gone in mentally debilitating
disease, or just old age and memory loss, mistakes Dicey for
Daisy, a woman whose name does not appear in any of the official
genealogies of the kin. He scrawls a note and presses it upon
Dicey. Outside the sickroom she opens it and reads: "'River—
Daisy—Midnight—Please'" (148). Although her name rhymes
with Daisy's, Dicey seems to find her echo-self as the object of
desperate passion to be an uncomfortable position. Resisting the
call to passion in Felix's note, Dicey moves back to her extra-kin
world, the world where her fiancé is her sweetheart (155) and
lovers live happily ever after in a world where love is less physical, less feral.

"Ladies in Spring," sometimes underrated as a "Mississippi"
place and folk story, actually plays the same theme of wins and
losses in love as the "sophisticated," non-Mississippi stories in *The
Bride of the* Innisfallen.

Dewey Coker, the naive point of view character of "Ladies
in Spring," is a country boy upon whom lessons and signifi-

cances register but lay dormant until his own experience, presumably acquired with age, makes it possible for him to interpret the central lessons of his life. Those lessons concerned his father, Blackie, and his mother—between whom there is a grudge relationship—and Opal, a strange girl whom Dewey meets while fishing with his father. It does not occur to Dewey until fifteen years later that, on the day his father had liberated him from school to take him fishing, it had been Opal in the woods who had plaintively called out Blackie's name (99). All of the adults knew the scenario, and lived with it—his father with blithe unconcern, his mother with gritted resentment. Neither readers nor Dewey himself can be sure of what "happens" in "Ladies in Spring." Has Blackie used his son to break off a relationship with Opal because he is too much a coward to do so face to face? Has Opal showed up at the fishing spot by her own design but without Blackie's knowledge? How much does the rainmaker/postmistress Hattie Purcell know? Answers lie in the territory introduced by "Circe" and "No Place for You, My Love."

"Going to Naples" serves as a case in point for the bright critical future for *The Bride of the* Innisfallen, a book that started off perplexing reviewers. Earlier literary critics like Ruth Vande Kieft looked for thematic connections to traditional interpretive schemes: the innocence-to-experience structure, for example. Kreyling and Polk approached the story with more nuanced attention to verbal and imagery patterns. A more contemporary group of critics, employing the insights of feminist criticism have corrected earlier assessments and found coherent structures of meaning where before only "obscurity" had been suspected. Dawn

Trouard's reading of "Going to Naples" is representative of this new departure.[11]

Exposing blind spots in interpretations of "Going to Naples" that see it as a story that celebrates a woman who can dance in the so-called "defeat" of her reachings for love in another (male), Trouard reveals "its own . . . impulse . . . pressure . . . and fulfillment" in Gabriella Serto's acceptance of herself alone as the territory of her happiness. As the final story in the sequence of composition of the seven stories in *The Bride of the* Innisfallen, "Going to Naples" marks the fine line between surrendering to defeated passion and remaining faithful to one's passion because it is one's own whether or not it succeeds in possessing an object. Gabriella Serto's joyous dance at the end of the story (and collection) reflects Virgie Rainey's ecstatic immersion in the Big Black River at the climax of *The Golden Apples.* Both women have found that they are sufficient within themselves for the joy of living.

Although *The Bride of the* Innisfallen mystified and displeased critics in 1955 who were, most recently, accustomed to Welty's broad humor or, earlier in her career, the critical commonplace of author and work as "southern," these stories strike more widely and deeply. More widely because they define Welty as a woman writing (not merely a woman writer), and a woman writing claims more scope than a southern writer. More deeply because the technique she uses—using a narrative pattern from story to story, planting variation in each of the stories to "raise" the pattern in different aspects, exploring sex and psyche—challenges the reader to rethink his or her assumptions about the creating power of the word, the image, the sentence, the story—fiction itself.

CHAPTER EIGHT

Losing Battles

Losing Battles, published in 1970, was a kind of resurrection in Welty's career. She had not published a book in fifteen years, and nearly every knowledgeable reviewer took advantage of the publication of *Losing Battles* to reassess Welty's career and welcome her back among the living. For a writer who so often employs the myth of Persephone, the irony must have been bittersweet.

Louis D. Rubin Jr., closely tracking Welty's career within the larger confines of southern literature, announced her resurrection succinctly:

> Miss Welty when last seen, in 1955, published *The Bride of the* Innisfallen, her third collection of short stories (fourth if you count *The Golden Apples*). Thereafter, and for fifteen years, silence, the only exceptions being a little privately-printed essay, *Place in Fiction,* and a few magazine pieces. So it has been a long time between books.[1]

Understandable anxiety for a new Welty book prompted Rubin to lump Welty's three *New Yorker* stories ("Where Is the Voice Coming From?" "The Demonstrators," and "The Optimist's Daughter") under the heading "a few magazine pieces," but his statement is representative of critical greetings for *Losing Battles*. Fifteen years was a large gap in the career of a writer who had risen to important status in the prime of her career, then more or less dropped off the literary radar scope. Her reappearance was cause for celebration of a talent many had thought extinct.

James Boatwright was one of the celebrants. In his front-page review in *The New York Times Book Review,* he called Welty's new novel "a major work of the imagination and a gift to cause general rejoicing."[2] Boatwright used his review to scan backward over Welty's career, implying that *Losing Battles* might be her swan song. Reynolds Price, calling Welty's novel a "frightening gift," compared it to *The Tempest, The Winter's Tale,* and *War and Peace.*[3]

If many reviews were celebratory, there were at least as many valedictions to what many thought a superannuated genre—if not to an outdated writer. Of the latter reviews, Jonathan Yardley's "The Last Good One?" with its conspicuous question mark, is the most provocative. If Yardley praised *Losing Battles,* he did so mournfully, for he saw the long, family-chronicle (a.k.a. southern) novel as an obsolete genre no longer capable of addressing the issues of the present moment:

> If I am correct in guessing that it is a work motivated in large measure by nostalgia, then it is a nostalgia not merely for a lost South but for a lost Southern literature. Undoubtedly someone will come along to prove me wrong, but I suspect that *Losing Battles* is the last "Southern novel"—or should I say the last good one.[4]

Joyce Carol Oates's "Eudora's Web," though praising Welty by ranking her with Jane Austen, nevertheless finds *Losing Battles* something of a fossil:

In 1970 the concerns of *Losing Battles* are extinct. The large, happy family and its outdoor feast are extinct; the loyalty to a postage-stamp corner of the world is extinct; the unquestioning Christian faith, the complex and yet very simple web of relationships that give these people their identities, binding them to a particular past and promising for them a particular, inescapable future: all extinct.[5]

Louis Rubin's essay-review "Everything Brought Out in the Open: Eudora Welty's *Losing Battles,*" quoted above, refutes Oates's assertions point for point. John W. Aldridge's "Eudora Welty: The Metamorphosis of a Southern Lady Writer" is more ambivalent. If Aldridge praises Welty and *Losing Battles* in particular, it is because the Mississippi writer found a way to write southern literature in an idiom Faulkner had *not* pioneered. It took her almost thirty years, Aldridge calculates, but Welty finally broke the spell.[6]

Suzanne Marrs, in *The Welty Collection,* lists seventy-three reviews held by the Mississippi Department of Archives and History, and this collection does not include reviews from smaller outlets. *Losing Battles* is far and away Welty's most widely reviewed book, and the range of opinion in the reviews amounts almost to a referendum on Welty's entire achievement: themes, influences, growth and metamorphosis, and ultimate ranking in the canon.

As is usually the case, longer critical essays have moved outward along lines sketched in early reviews. Yardley's review, arguing that as fine as *Losing Battles* might be, it is a good example of an obsolete form, is implicitly taken up by Carol S. Manning in "*Losing Battles:* Tall Tale and Comic Epic," chapter 7 in her book-length study of Welty's work *With Ears Opening Like Morning Glories: Eudora Welty and the Love of Storytelling.* Manning cuts the ground out from under Yardley's criticism by arguing that *Losing Battles* is a conscious parody of the southern novel and must, therefore, be read *not* as a relic of an outdated genre but has the harbinger of a new wave. Manning reads the characters in *Losing Battles* as parodic of the heroic characters common to traditional southern fiction, and the eroded kinship system as parodic of the southern theme of community:

> That Welty [Manning continues] should come to parody a tradition of Southern literature which not only was firmly established but, according to some critics, even dying by the time she began *Losing Battles* should not be surprising. She has always had a parodic streak, a consequence in part of her thorough acquaintance with and enjoyment of many narrative and literary traditions. (142)

For readers uncomfortable with parody as the final word—for parody sometimes seems to unravel more than it stitches together—there are more affirmative thematic readings of *Losing Battles*. Kreyling's interpretation in *Eudora Welty's Achievement of Order* (1980) finds a kind of affirmation in the novel's balancing of the claims of myth and history to the order of human experience. Vande Kieft (1986) finds a similar truce.

The long, painstaking, and complex composition of the novel and the ramifications for our understanding of its structure and meaning are explored by Suzanne Marrs in *The Welty Collection* (1988). Marrs's critique, based on examination of the extant drafts and revisions of the novel's many parts, exposes the evolution of characters and events in the novel that readers comprehend only as finished products (18–19). It is evident from Marrs's work that completing *Losing Battles* was equivalent to scaling Mount Everest.

The passage of time between *The Bride of the* Innisfallen and *Losing Battles,* however, remains crucial. Welty's record as one of American literature's finest short-story writers would not seem to predict a long, choral novel such as *Losing Battles.* Although two additional short stories responding to the violent upheavals in the South over Civil Rights, "Where Is the Voice Coming From?" (1963) and "The Demonstrators" (1968)—the latter the winner of an O. Henry Prize—continued recognizable patterns in her writing, "The Optimist's Daughter" was as yet a long *New Yorker* story. *Losing Battles* seemed an anomaly.

Losing Battles closely resembled nothing Welty had yet written. Although it has been compared to *Delta Wedding,* in that both novels celebrate family in the midst of an affirmative ritual of kinship, in structure it is nothing like the thickly brocaded narrative of the earlier novel. *Losing Battles* is almost exclusively dramatic dialogue, 436 pages of voices vying for narrative space and the reader's ear. Most of the "story" present in *Losing Battles* is embedded in the voices of one or more of the numerous characters gathered at the Vaughn-Renfro-Beecham reunion. It is as if the monologic narrative of *The*

Ponder Heart had been broken, each one of the numerous characters given her or his own story, *and then* those stories had been disassembled again and interwoven piece by piece.

The conditions under which Welty wrote the novel are of some help in understanding the kind of work it is. In 1955, in the midst of *The Ponder Heart* whirlwind on Broadway and as Welty was assembling and polishing the stories for *The Bride of the* Innisfallen, her mother went to New Orleans for eye surgery. Mrs. Welty's vision had been deteriorating for some time in the early 1950s; being unable to fend for herself was a blow to a widow of twenty years who had lived a life of fierce self-reliance. The surgery did not correct the vision problem, and Mrs. Welty's physical and psychological health continued to deteriorate excruciatingly slowly.

Eudora Welty, used to traveling as her means made it possible, found herself obliged to become nurse to her mother and to earn money for household and medical expenses. Hired caregivers did not work out; at least one nursing home was tried and rejected. Between caring for her mother and working at short- and medium-term literary jobs, Welty found replenishment in writing bits and pieces of "a long story about the country." Drawing upon scenes and sounds and characters from her itinerant photographic work in the early 1930s, Welty established a northeast Mississippi backwoods place, Banner, and a couple of interconnected clans, Beechams and Vaughns and Renfros, to people it. She would write scenes or patches of scenes and store them in shoe boxes by character or topic. She had no specific end in sight when she undertook this project, no final shape which she was gradually filling. In a sense, Welty was writing against the grain of the craft she had perfected over two decades. Life conditions, however, made the open-ended process necessary.

Welty's brother Walter died in 1959; he was forty-three. On January 20, 1966, her mother, aged eighty-three, died. Four days later her brother Edward, the brother with whom she had the closer and more hilarious relationship (see her *One Writer's Beginnings*), also died; he was fifty-four. Suddenly, Welty was alone with only memories of her immediate family. A draft of a long story or novella about the death of parents and the impact on the surviving child ("Poor Eyes," the title of this draft, was to become *The Optimist's Daughter* [1969; 1972]) was complete by the middle of the following year, 1967. While "Poor Eyes" stewed in Welty's revisioning imagination and in the scheduling plans of *The New Yorker,* the author went to the shoe boxes and began to "quilt" *Losing Battles* into a continuous narrative.

Like Samuel Clemens's *Adventures of Huckleberry Finn* (1885), showing in its finished form the fissures of disparate sessions of composition, Welty's *Losing Battles* displays in its published form the fault lines that developed over the fifteen years of its evolution. The novel is divided, even against itself, by theme and structure. On the level of theme, *Losing Battles* affirms the values of loyalty to family, persistence in place, guardianship of traditions. As the kin celebrates its wholeness at a birthday party for Granny Vaughn, ninety years old the dry August day the novel opens, narrative structure follows nature's cycle from dawn to nightfall to the morning of the following day. Individual narratives tug against the narrative of the natural order. Willie Trimble's story of Julia Mortimer's death in Alliance, a town across the Bywy River from Banner, triggers Miss Lexie Renfro's more complicated story, which in turn dislodges another story from Granny, and then a confession from Uncle Nathan. Each of the individual narratives is pieced into the "quilted" whole, but the whole itself has a narrative pattern that tends to negate the importance of human individuality.

The conflict of forms can be seen another way. The stories narrated by the series of voices at the reunion, if they were to be lifted from context and slightly remolded, would be familiar in structure as versions of perennially popular tales. Manning's detection of literary parody can be extended. Julia Mortimer's compressed life story—house arrest under the control of Lexie, desperate attempts to smuggle communications to the outside world—resembles the madwoman-in-the-attic plot of captivity and hoped-for release that the Brontes often used. The story of Dearman, the clear-cutter of Mississippi forests, who falls for Julia but is then murdered in a crime of passion by Nathan Vaughn (who then in self-inflicted punishment severs his right hand), borrows much from Faulknerian gothic. Judge Oscar Moody's story of his relationship with Julia Mortimer and the impact of her example on his life and career recalls the plots of Cather's *My Ántonia* and *A Lost Lady.* Cather has long been an underreported "influence" on Welty.

The point, however, is not that *Losing Battles* is an album of Welty's favorite influences, sources, or originals. Rather, as much as the theme of the novel is a plea for the stability of family identity, perseverance in place against the inevitably victorious forces of modernity, the literariness of the novel diverts attention away from theme and toward form. The several embedded narratives and various narrative shapes reminiscent of other works disperse linear momentum into spatial form.

Welty launches *Losing Battles* with a simile in which the literary and the natural compete:

> When the rooster crowed, the moon had still not left the world but was going down on flushed cheek, one day short of the full. A long thin cloud crossed it slowly, drawing itself out like a name being called. The air changed, as if a mile or so away a wooden door had swung open, and a smell, more of warmth than wet, from a river at low stage, moved upward into the clay hills that stood in darkness. (3)

Although more homemade than T. S. Eliot's highly refined waste land image of the evening sky like a patient etherized upon a table, Welty's imagery is similar in thematic and stylistic effects. The thematic effect evokes a natural universe oblivious to the human, against the backdrop of which the human action takes place. Eliot's imagery argues that human endeavors are tawdry or futile; Welty is more generous. The stylistic effect of her language is to accentuate the differences between the lyrical, metaphorical narrative voice and the folksy, matter-of-fact idiom of the human characters. *Losing Battles* takes place in a rural world on the verge of exhaustion, a pastoral bower just about counted out, but the literary perspective on that world rich is metaphor, image, and formal range. Situated within the cacophony of contesting human voices, the elaborate use of imagery suggests the separateness of humanity at odds with nature. Welty's choice of waste land imagery (drought, dried-up rivers, drooping vegetation, ubiquitous dust) further suggests the isolation of mankind even though the assembled families insist on the need to hang on.

Part 1 of the novel arranges for the many guests to arrive, each car trailing clouds of symbolic dust into the Renfro compound. One after another the guests comment on the new tin roof on the Renfro house and ask about Jack, the oldest son, sentenced to Parchman Prison Farm two years ago. Granny's birthday is one day shy of his scheduled release, but the clan is intent on conjuring his arrival. As if to underline the magical powers of the family en masse, Jack bounds into the compound full of ebullient good cheer. That cheer gradually ebbs as he is told of the sacrifice he has suffered in absentia: his horse, Dan, has died; his truck has been sold to his rival; his grandfather Vaughn has died without seeing his grandson again. But now that their messiah has, symbolically, arrived, all are confident that the family's fortunes will be reversed even though Jack's own fate seems to be to lose one by one each of his treasures.

Part 2 brings the nemesis of the family, Judge Oscar Moody, who sentenced Jack to Parchman, into the plot. Jack has already helped him free his car from a ditch, not knowing that the man he helped was the judge who had sentenced him. When the family tells Jack the news, he resolves to find Moody again and undo his Good Samaritan act. The unrescue is narrated in slapstick comedy style. Jack, his wife, Gloria, and the baby he had never seen until this day, Lady May, are surprised by the Moody's Buick. Lady May, darting across the dirt road, causes the judge to swerve. The Buick sprints up an incline to Banner Top and there comes to rest propped on one of Uncle Nathan Beecham's evangelizing signs (the paint on it still tacky), its engine running, rear wheels spinning, radiator dangling over the precipice. The only thing keeping the Buick from toppling is the ballast provided by Jack's bumpkin foil, Aycock Comfort, in the backseat. Both Aycock and Jack had walked off from Parchman on the same day; now Aycock is enjoined to stay in the backseat of the judge's Buick lest the distribution of weight be thrown off. With no place to go and no one to help them with the teetering car (a series of potential helpers arrive, but in absurdist Marx-Brothers discussions each one finds a compelling reason not to help the judge and Mrs. Moody), Jack invites his nemesis to join the family at the reunion.

Part 3 admits the judge into the reunion, over vociferous but short-lived protest. The various members of the family surreptitiously rejoice in the presence of the outsider, for in Mr. and Mrs. Moody there is a new audience for their old story: the world according to Beecham. The juxtaposition of concerted human voices (affirming oneness and camaraderie) and the content of the story they tell creates torquing thematic tension in the novel for the first time. Introducing themselves to the town-dwelling Presbyterians, the Moodys, the Beechams essentially stake their dwindling rural fortunes against the rest of the outside world. The motif of "losing battle" is heard from the lips of the battlers themselves:

"We're relying on Jack now. He'll haul us out of our misery, and we thought he was going to haul us with that do-

all truck." Uncle Curtis's long face cracked open into
its first smile. "Since all my boys done up and left my
farm." . . .

"It's the same old story," said Uncle Dolphus. "It's the
fault of the land going back on us, treating us the wrong
way. There's been too much of the substance washed
away to grow enough to eat any more." (194)

The impenetrable separateness of the human and the natural
expressed earlier in the novel through stylistic elements
(metaphor and simile) is here corroborated by the voices themselves. It is not, however, only a natural clash; it is human and
intrafamilial as well. All of Uncle Curtis's sons have left; were
nature to return the land to pastoral fruitfulness there would not
be anyone to accept the gift. Human life is an eternally losing
battle.

Uncle Curtis's lament is not nearly as disturbing as the story
of the desertion of the Beecham children by their mother and
father, a story that their collective voices tell the judge and his
wife. Apparently deciding to abandon their seven children, the
parents raced away from home only to plunge to their deaths in
the Bywy River (for once, running high [215]) when their carriage plummeted through a gap in the bridge's floorboards.
"'Somebody was running away from us children, that's what I
believed at the time and still believe,' said Uncle Noah Webster"
(217). Confusion and guilt hang over the telling of the parents'
desertion. No one in the Beecham clan has an answer. "'Take me
back to the bridge a minute. What errand was they both so bent
on when they hitched and cut loose from the house so early and

drove out of sight of Grandpa and Granny, children and all, that morning?' It was Aunt Beck with the gentle voice who prodded"(218). She gets no answer; thematically, then, at the origin of the myth of intimately shared family joy lurks its antithesis: desertion anxiety. This story, like many others told of and by the assembled kin, is never resolved.

Part 4 is rich in thematic incidents. Interpreters of *Losing Battles* have found what seems to be the treasury of the novel's meanings here. The first to materialize is the family's collective conclusion, from bits and pieces of evidence divulged by Granny, that Gloria Short, Jack Renfro's wife and the mother of Lady May, is in fact his cousin—the illegitimate daughter of Sam Dale Beecham (deceased) and Rachel Sojourner, even lower on the social scale than the Beechams. Gloria rejects all the anecdotal "evidence" and discloses in the process that Julia Mortimer, under whom she apprenticed as a teacher, had warned her not to become involved with Jack Renfro lest degrees of blood relation be violated. Gloria had stubbornly closed her ears, both to warnings against breaking the customs of marriage *and* to calls to dedicate herself to teaching, which would have meant celibacy. The family, though, is convinced of her membership, and they "baptize" Gloria as a Beecham by force-feeding her hunks of warm watermelon (269). Gloria will not bend in the kinship orgy, and is proud of her resistance.

Judge Moody's presence in Beecham territory is explained when Willy Trimble, the local jack-of-all-trades, shows up with a coffin that he had made for Julia Mortimer, only to have it rejected as not fine enough by those who had taken over her funeral. The judge is in Banner country because a desperate letter from the schoolteacher had summoned him. He is too late to help, but not too late for Julia Mortimer's funeral. Lexie's tongue is now loosened. Stitching a rip in Gloria's dress, Lexie tells the story of nursing Julia Mortimer in her final days. She had left the woman to come to the reunion, and Julia had been found dying on the road by Willy Trimble. Shame is not among Lexie's emotions, however, and she keeps up a continuous barrage-narrative of the suffering she inflicted on Julia Mortimer. Lexie withheld reading material, then paper and pencil. She lied when she told Julia she had mailed her letters, and destroyed those the teacher received. Thematically, this episode (272–88) depicts the family as relentlessly oppressive to the individual. Whenever Julia, the thematic representative of the individual, seeks some form of expression for that individuality, the clan slams the request with flat refusal—and thinks no less of itself for doing so.

Welty constructs the episode, however, so that attention is not exclusively directed toward Lexie. Welty's dramatic style is vividly in evidence here, for Gloria's attention to Lexie's story is palpable even though the words on the pages are nearly all Lexie's. Gloria is foregrounded as if she were an actor on a stage while another, playing Lexie, is speaking. What Lexie says is chilling enough, and the family's response is just as unsympathetic and benighted. While telling her gruesome tale, however, Lexie holds Gloria captive by stitching her dress. Gloria must listen to the suffering she in large part caused by abandoning Julia Mortimer for marriage and motherhood. As Lexie's tale builds to her torture of Julia Mortimer, Gloria's off-center reaction becomes more important. "'Stop quivering,'" Lexie orders Gloria. Beechams, Renfros, and Vaughns must conclude that Gloria is just fidgeting under Lexie's protracted rough needlework, but the readers can see the fuller meaning of Lexie's "needling" (277). Lexie climaxes her tale by telling how she first locked Julia Mortimer in her own house when she wanted to get out to touch the world, and then resorted to tying her to her own bed (278). Telling how Julia had asked Lexie to get in touch with Gloria, Lexie adds psychological torture to the physical by telling her patient: "'Oh, she's just forgotten you, Julia, like everybody else has'" (279).

The Beecham clan, paradoxically representing the positive values of communal living, applauds Lexie's cruelty. After all, the schoolteacher had been nothing but a scourge to them. Judge Moody, silent during Lexie's sordid narrative, "lifted a face strained around the eyes, filling now with a martyred look" as he adds his contribution to the telling of Julia Mortimer's life (290). Discovering her last will and testament, he reads it out to the assembled reunion. None of the instructions left behind will, as it turns out, be fulfilled. Classes will not go on as usual; Julia will not be buried under the front step to Banner School; she will not have a "plain coffin, no fuss" (291). She seems to have known in advance that each of her wishes would be denied, each small battle lost as the big one was also lost.

Judge Moody produces an earlier letter from Julia, a letter that the schoolteacher had spirited out of the house through Lexie's blockade. Julia Mortimer's summons to the judge, a former student, had of course arrived late and he had delayed even longer in answering it. When the judge reads the text of the letter to the reunion, readers of the novel have the nearest thing to a thematic billboard:

"Oscar, it's only now, when I've come to lie flat on my
back, that I've had it driven in on me—the reason I never
could win for good is that both sides were using the same
tactics. Very likely true of all wars. A teacher teaches and
a pupil learns or fights against learning with the same force
behind him. It's the survival instinct. It's a mighty power,
it's an iron weapon while it lasts. It's the desperation of
staying alive against all odds that keeps both sides encour-
aged. But the side that gets licked gets to the truth first.
When the battle's over, something may dawn there—with
no help from the teacher, no help from the pupil, no help
from the book. After the lessons give out and the eyes give
out, when memory's trying its best to cheat you—to lie
and hide from you, and you know some day it could even
run off and leave you, there's just one thing, one reliable
thing left." (298)

Julia Mortimer's letter goes on to tell her former pupil what is left:
the simple record of the witnessed fact instead of the embroidered
and self-serving myth of the collective group. She does not tell the
judge the fact in her letter, although she intimates that it has to do
with a child, and the judge arrives too late to get the answer in her
living voice (300). Is it Gloria's child? Gloria herself?

Part 5 begins with nightfall; the stylistic stage setting of the
opening of the novel, and of the day of the Beecham reunion, is
reprised for the night "act":

Suddenly the moonlit world was doused; lights hard as
pick-axe blows drove down from every ceiling and the

> roof of the passage, cutting the house and all in it away,
> leaving them an island now on black earth, afloat in night,
> and nowhere, with only each other. In that first moment
> every face, white-lit but with its caves of mouth and eyes
> opened wide, black with the lonesomeness and hilarity of
> survival, showed its kinship to Uncle Nathan's, the face
> that floated over theirs. For the first time, all talk was cut
> off, and no baby offered to cry. Silence came travelling in
> on solid, man-made light. (312)

Exposed in one Edvard Munch-like instant of panic, the family
resumes talk lest they be engulfed in oblivion. The night stories
they tell are more problematic than those of the daytime in that
they probe more deeply into the unspoken and unresolved anxi-
eties which their concerted and constantly chirping voices are
designed to mute. That Nathan Beecham's face is the one that
hovers over the family's like a Blakean icon further suggests
that the wandering outcast, not the tightly clustering brood, is the
hub of the family.

Judge Moody's tongue is loosened after night falls; after he
has spoken for the dead schoolteacher, he speaks for himself. His
voice is the voice of the law, abstract and rational, thinking from
written statutes to particular cases. He clashes with the family's
legislative practice, which flows in the opposite direction: empirical and associational, taking the particular case in and of itself
and rejecting the written statute altogether. The parties had
argued this ground once before: if the judge had just known the
particular facts of the case of *Jack Renfro v. Curly Stovall* as
the kin knew them, no one would have had to go to Parchman.

Under the colors of family narration, "evidence" and "facts" blur into a continuous reality.

The marriage of Gloria and Jack brings the conflict of folk and state to a sharp edge. The state presumes an interest in regulating marriage between relatives within certain degrees of kinship. That interest lies in ensuring the genetic "health" of the population at large. The family clings to its interest in redoubling the layers of kinship; that Gloria and Jack might be first cousins is far from a danger to them. The judge argues the law to the family, but he makes little headway. In the end he is defeated by the unarguable fact of Lady May (the child simply cannot be transformed into an abstraction) and by the refusal of all assembled to see her in terms of something referred to as "the law." Gloria speaks for them:

> "I didn't have to believe Miss Julia Mortimer if I didn't want to," Gloria repeated. Then she came headlong at Judge Moody, holding her baby bucketed, and Lady May's little legs stuck out pointed at his head like two guns even though she was asleep. "Is that what's at the end of your Sunday errand, sir? Did you come all the way to Banner to make Jack's baby and mine null and void, and take Jack away from me again?" (320–21)

Moody takes refuge in the ambiguity of the evidence, hearsay and unsigned postcards, and suspends his position as voice of the law. He does suggest that Jack and Gloria move across the state line to Alabama, where such unions as theirs *might be* recognized under the state law. But this move would destroy the solidarity of the family, and Jack refuses (321).

As the night deepens, so too do the stories. Granny tells a story that links Dearman, the long-dead lumberman whose gangs had clear-cut a good deal of the state, with the Beecham family through Miss Julia Mortimer, a boarder with the family early in her career. Like a Faulknerian Snopes, Dearman entered the community and ended up owning most of the worthwhile capital in timber acreage and other businesses. "'We didn't even get the sawdust!' cried Uncle Noah Webster to his wife" (341). Unlike a Snopes, though, Dearman is mortal and Uncle Nathan confesses to killing him (344). Nathan's exile is self-imposed punishment.

The reunion ends with the departure of most of the guests except those, like the Moodys, who have no place else to go. As the house settles down and night weighs heavily, those left standing seek what solace they can. Jack and Gloria make love as a way of enduring the present under the shadow of oblivion. Vaughn, Jack's younger brother, freed paradoxically to develop his own personality when Jack was sentenced to Parchman, comes into his own as the incipient individual ready and willing to flee the clustering family to the interior life symbolized in the school: "He so loved Banner School that he would have beaten sunup and driven there now, if the doors had had any way of opening for him" (364). Covered by night, Vaughn revisits the Moody Buick, knowing in his heart that he could have rescued it but had to defer to his older, but not necessarily more clever, brother. He hides the Banner school bus so that he can be the driver in the morning, hoping to thwart Jack's repossession of priv-

ilege. When he returns to the house, the claustrophobic nature
of the family closes down upon him. Stepping over kin with
almost every pace, he looks for some private niche in which to
sleep. Before he can find it, however, he comes face to face
with the problem of kin, its overpowering adhesiveness:

> Then all of a sudden there came through the passage a
> current of air. A door swung open in Vaughn's face and
> there was Granny, tiny in her bed in full lamplight. For a
> moment the black bearskin on the floor by the bed shone
> red-haired, live enough to spring at him. After the moon-
> light and the outdoors, the room was as yellow and close
> as if he and Granny were embedded together in a bar of
> yellow soap.
>
> "Take off your hat," Granny's mouth said. "And
> climb in wi' me." (366)

Vaughn, wearing his grandfather's hat, flees from the threat of
a more intimate connection to kin than the one he already has.
Incest had already proved no problem to the clan in the case of
Gloria, but Vaughn seems to want no part of doubled connection. Vaughn's reaction echoes the anxiety of Laura in *Delta
Wedding*. Like Laura, Vaughn is troubled that the elders cannot
seem to distinguish him from long-dead members of the group:
"'She didn't know who I was,' he told himself, running. And
then, 'She didn't care'" (366).

Part 6 takes up the morning after the reunion and shifts the
novel's ground from the Beecham farm to the town where the
funeral of Julia Mortimer is being conducted. The salvaging of

the Moody's touring car is taken care of in a screwball comedy sequence that equals, and structurally balances, the placing of the car there in part 1. Jack's truck reappears, then is towed away. Dan, the horse who was thought to have been rendered, comes back, like Lazarus, to rejoin the living. Romance is intimated between Curly Stovall, arch foe to the Renfro clan, and Jack's sister Ella Fay. The clan cannot protect itself against infiltration by its worst enemies. In the midst of this welter of goings-on, Julia Mortimer is buried point for point against her expressed wishes, but buried nevertheless with such an influx of exotic outsiders as Banner and Alliance had never before seen.

The final scene is reserved for Jack and Gloria. Walking to the funeral through Banner Cemetery, Jack narrates a tour of the graves, calling out the names of the dead kin and the places ready for the living. Kin is all one pulsating group to him, dead or alive, while Gloria futilely keeps up a chorus of dissent, planning for separation, a house of their own, distance between their new family and the old one. Jack is oblivious. Gloria insists:

He stood in her arms without answering, and she dropped her own voice to a whisper. "If we could stay this way always—build us a little two-room house, where nobody in the world could find us—"

He drew her close, as if out of sudden danger. (431)

This tableau sums up *Losing Battles:* Locked in a loving-hating embrace, the impulses to separation and connection, self and kin, keep the human race in an unresolved rhythm. Gloria seems to represent the self and the self's conception of mortal time encompassed temporarily in one's own flesh; Jack embodies the kin group's different sense of time, closing on one member only to open for another. There is a kind of immortality in Jack's alternative, but it comes with a price.

Dedicated to the memory of her brothers who died while she was writing *Losing Battles,* and tinged as well with the presence of her mother in several of the female characters, Welty's novel thematically gravitates to the meanings of kinship, the dual identity of every human being as both autonomous self and obligated brother or sister, child or parent. Critical treatments of *Losing Battles* generally tend to thematic studies and have, wisely, steered clear of the biographical. But Welty had a mother and two brothers when she began writing the novel and was alone when it was published. The puzzling condition of the survivor must surely lie behind the final scenes of the novel: Julia's funeral, Jack's guided tour of the cemetery, and his enlivening rendition of "Bringing in the Sheaves" with which the novel ends. The predicament of the survivor would be the central concern of Welty's next two books, the inseparable pair of *The Optimist's Daughter* and *One Writer's Beginnings.*

CHAPTER NINE

The Optimist's Daughter and *One Writer's Beginnings*

The Optimist's Daughter (1972) and *One Writer's Beginnings* (1984) are so closely related that discussion of one inevitably flows into discussion of the other. Welty's last novel, completed in novella form just months after the death of her mother in 1966, centers around a widowed daughter, Laurel McKelva Hand, summoned home to Mount Salus, Mississippi, when her father enters the hospital for eye surgery. The father's subsequent death—not, it seems, from complications of the surgery—throws the daughter into a maelstrom of identity and memory confusion: Was her father's second marriage, to a tacky typist, somehow her fault? Was it her mother's? Did Laurel leave family and home-town because of love for her own dead husband? Or did she leave to escape suffocating layers of town and family? Was she a good daughter to her mother, to her father? Welty's mem-oir of growing up in Jackson follows much the same path, but from an autobiographical direction. Both her parents are promi-nent in her memoir, although her mother takes the spotlight. Readers cannot help but read both mother-daughter relationships as, somehow, continuous.

Before the publication of the Welty's autobiographical mem-oir, most critical discussions of *The Optimist's Daughter* intuited an autobiographical accent to the novel, especially to the central family triangle of Laurel and her parents, Judge Clinton McKelva and his wife, Becky, who has been dead several years when the action of the novel begins. Except for readers familiar with some of the facts of the author's off-page life, few could go beyond the assertion that the mother-daughter relationship was crucial to the character of Laurel and her struggle to live with the guilt of not being able to save either of her parents, or her long-dead husband, from inevitable death. Although Jack Renfro sang joyously in his losses at the conclusion of *Losing Battles,* being a survivor was harder for Laurel to bear and to understand. In the absence of anything like the "facts" later to be supplied by *One Writer's Beginnings,* reviewers and critics of *The Optimist's Daughter* saw the novel as a fable of the survivor, most often a fable of the artist as survivor—for Laurel is "artist" insofar as her profession in the novel (designer of curtains for theater companies) qualifies her as artist in general.

Writing a novel so unlike *Losing Battles* as to seem to be by another author was the best "revenge" on critics, such as Jonathan Yardley and Joyce Carol Oates (see the previous chapter), who had pronounced Welty and her métier "extinct" with the appearance of *Losing Battles.* Reviews of *The Optimist's Daughter* were uniformly good, and the novel won the Pulitzer Prize.

Before *One Writer's Beginnings,* critical essays on *The Optimist's Daughter* were usually sparked by the confrontation between Laurel and her father's second wife, Fay Chisom, over the "desecration" of Becky's breadboard. Does Fay "win" the exchange by virtue of her hardy survival instinct that life belongs to the living? After all, she reminds Laurel, who insists the breadboard is symbolic, a breadboard is for making bread and Becky is "'not making it now'" (173). As for Laurel's late husband, Philip Hand (killed in the Pacific in World War II), who made the breadboard: "'What has *he* got to do with it? . . . He's dead, isn't he?'" (177). Psychologically speaking, Fay travels light, and there is something to be said for minimizing the burden of the grave.

Most critics give the palm to Laurel. In an early essay on the novel, "The Past Reexamined: *The Optimist's Daughter,*" Cleanth Brooks dismisses Fay as "a shallow little vulgarian," "white trash," "cheap, self-centered, aggressive, and completely unmannerly."[1] Laurel's surrender of the actual object of wood, the breadboard, is in Brooks's view a deeper affirmation of possession of the meaning it represents:

> So Laurel can now put her mother's scarred breadboard "down on the table where it belonged," forgoing the quixotic gesture of taking it along with her. All that she leaves behind—family, home, furnishings and all—is impervious to Fay and the future. What for her is precious in it is past any harm that can be done to it by anyone. She is now ready to take her plane back to Chicago and her job.[2]

Reynolds Price, writing about the version of "The Optimist's Daughter" published in *The New Yorker* (March 15, 1969), reached a similar conclusion, complicated only by his sense that Laurel acted not only for the self charged to remember the past but also for the artist, for Welty herself as artist:

> For there is at the end, each time I've reached it, a complicated sense of joy. Simple exhilaration in the courage and

skill of the artist, quite separate from the tragic burden of the action. Joy that a piece of credible life has been displayed to us fully and, in the act, fully explained (I take Laurel's understanding to be also the author's and ours; there can be no second meaning, no resort to attempts to discredit Laurel's vision.)[3]

Most critics followed the lines pointed out by Brooks and Price—at least until the publication of *One Writer's Beginnings.* Laurel acts for genuine memory, not kitsch nostalgia that needs the past frozen like the woolly mammoth in a glacier of memory. And, acknowledging Price's added layer of meaning, Laurel acts as and for the artist: *The Optimist's Daughter* is in that sense reflective of Welty's vocation, if not of her life.

With the publication of *One Writer's Beginnings* twelve years after the novel, readers have been given what is essentially a close, if not exact, annotation by the author to her earlier novel. In fact, the two texts work in tandem oblivious to the actual sequence of chronological relationship: the earlier informs the latter, and vice versa. The central triangular relationship of the novel—mother, father, daughter—reappears in *One Writer's Beginnings* with the daughter's relationship to herself through her profession as artist—the writer who begins—more distinctly clarified than it is in *The Optimist's Daughter.* Reciprocally, the relationship between Becky and Laurel in the novel, with much of its emotional currents kept at a deliberate, low frequency, is loosened in the memoir as Welty tentatively explores the psychological control through guilt that her mother exercised over daughter in particular and family in general. The daughter's acknowledgment of guilt in the memoir rebounds upon the novel, setting loose in the character of Fay and in the bitter relationship between Fay and Laurel notes of discord the novel strives to mute. "There can be no second meaning," Price declared; but he had not allowed for the author herself supplying it.

Carolyn G. Heilbrun's study of women's autobiography, *Writing a Woman's Life* (1988), lit the fuse to new and controversial "second meanings" to both the novel and the memoir. "There are four ways to write a woman's life," Heilbrun begins:

> the woman herself may tell it, in what she chooses to call an autobiography; she may tell it in what she chooses to call fiction; a biographer, woman or man, may write the woman's life in what is called a biography; or the woman may write her own life in advance of living it, unconsciously, and without recognizing or naming the process.[4]

It is the fourth category Heilbrun pursues, and Welty's *One Writer's Beginnings* is one of her chief vehicles for getting there. Yet it is not Heilbrun's admiration but her reservations that are important: "Yet I think there exists a real danger for women in books like Welty's in the nostalgia and romanticizing in which the author, and we in reading them, indulge" (13). The danger is that the woman's anger will go unexpressed and unknown by her readers. "I do not believe in the bittersweet quality of *One Writer's Beginnings,* nor do I suppose that the Eudora Welty there evoked could have written the stories and novels we have learned to celebrate," Heilbrun declares (14). Nostalgia, false or falsifying memory, is the virus, for it "imprisons" women who lack an artist's powers of veiled expression: "Nostalgia, particularly for childhood, is likely to be a mask for unrecognized anger" (15).

Heilbrun's thrusts have triggered responses by friend and foe, and changed the contours of Welty's reputation. Heilburn's reading of woman's autobiography, by revising our sense of such lives as Virginia Woolf's and Willa Cather's (two of the more significant "foremothers" to Welty), has forced us to reexamine interpretations of Welty's writing. In *Daughter of the Swan: Love and Knowledge in Eudora Welty's Fiction* (1994), for example, Gail L. Mortimer sees (almost certainly at Heilbrun's prompting) "a basic shift [with *The Optimist's Daughter*] in Welty's perspective on protective love" as a theme in her fiction (12). Not comfortable with Heilbrun's findings of "anger" in Welty, Mortimer still acknowledges the impact her rereadings have wrought on familiar literary works. Whether or not one agrees with Heilbrun's reception of Welty's memoir (and fiction), one must acknowledge that largely because of her skepticism there is much less fretting over an "extinct" southern writer.

The Optimist's Daughter opens in New Orleans during Mardi Gras. Laurel McKelva Hand, the only daughter of Judge Clinton McKelva and his first wife, Becky, has come hurriedly from her job and life in Chicago to a New Orleans hospital where her father is awaiting diagnosis and treatment for eye trouble. Along with the judge is his second wife, Fay, an early-fortyish woman who had caught the judge's eye in the secretarial pool at a bar association convention. They have been married about two years. Fay and the judge make a pair about as incongruous and troubling to the staid assumptions of the McKelva home community, Mount Salus, Mississippi, as Uncle Daniel and Bonnie Dee in *The Ponder Heart.* The disparity in their ages (about thirty years) mirrors the separation between Bonnie Dee and Daniel. Fay and the judge pointedly do not maintain the domestic sanctuary; Mount Salus buzzes with sightings of them in local restaurants. Fay's redecorating of the McKelva home has local tongues wagging as well.

If Fay and the judge invoke the star-crossed lovers of *The Ponder Heart,* then Laurel must take on Edna Earle's thankless role as third wheel. Laurel's anxiety is high but tightly wrapped. Her mother had gone to a hospital with similar eye complaints some years earlier, and she had died soon thereafter. The attending physician then, a former neighbor from Mount Salus, is the attending physician now, and Laurel fights off déjà vu with a desperation that comes through the words on the page. Moreover, Fay represents in woman and in wife all that Laurel (repeating Edna Earle's judgment) deplores: a kind of energetic vulgarity, sexuality, childlike self-centeredness, and an unreflective consumer appetite. Like Bonnie Dee, who bought electric appliances before the Ponder house was wired for power, Fay seems to charge first and ask questions later. She has come to New Orleans to shop and her husband's illness is postponing the pleasure of acquisition. Laurel's anxiety is topped off by the simple yet inescapable guilt that she chose to have her life away from Mount Salus; returning brings internal charges of disloyalty and abandonment.

Laurel did what Edna Earle only talked about, but she feels guilt for her choice. She cares for her father so intensely during his hospital incarceration as if she could expiate all of the guilt for leaving and the years living away in one concentrated penance. Heilbrun's detection of nostalgia-coated guilt works as well, perhaps better, in *The Optimist's Daughter* than it does in *One Writer's Beginnings.*

Laurel's father dies, and her unexpressed hope for forgiveness lives on in her wrestling with the personal and community memory of her parents. She has public rites of mourning to endure, and private harrowings (and revisions) of memory to face in rerelating herself to the actual things of her former life: letters, house, bedroom, breadboard. Edna Earle invented an ending to the story of Daniel and Bonnie Dee when she could no longer manage it from outside the narrative. Laurel is beset by the "inventedness" of the stories of herself and her parents shoved upon her by friends and her own eager memory.

Part 1 of the novel, set in the New Orleans hospital during Mardi Gras, introduces themes generated by Laurel's pent-up anxiety and guilt by way of symbols neatly embedded in exposition as "mere" detail. This is Welty's signature technique as a writer, and she exercises it with great skill, finesse, and economy in *The Optimist's Daughter.* An example of Welty's finesse occurs in the divided and delayed identification of the suit Laurel is wearing in the first scene of the novel. She has just flown in from Chicago, where the weather in March is much colder than it is so far south:

> She wore clothes of an interesting cut and texture, although her suit was wintry for New Orleans and had a wrinkle down the skirt. (3)

Her clothes translate symbolically as "out of place," and the wrinkle represents the controlled anxiety Laurel feels under the pressures of the situation. Poise and guilt identify Laurel's "wrinkled" character.

The inaugural mention of Laurel's suit, however, must not be forgotten when Welty returns to the issue of style on the day Laurel leaves Mount Salus several weeks later:

> Upstairs, Laurel folded her slacks and the wrinkled silk dress of last night into her case, dropped in the other few things she'd brought, and closed it. Then she bathed and dressed again in the Sibyl Connolly suit she'd flown down in. She was careful with her lipstick, and pinned her hair up for Chicago. (170)

Welty's finesse in managing the symbolic meanings of Laurel's fashion choices is admirable for the risk she takes in splitting the meanings between early and late in the novel. Like an echo, the late information about Laurel's suit reinforces the early mention. Donning the same suit she arrived in seems to express a wish or conviction on Laurel's part that the intervening rough experience has been tidied up, perhaps even erased, and that she can repossess the poise and self-control coded into the "Sibyl Connolly suit." Connolly, an Irish designer whose clothes became famous in the 1950s, was known for her use of native Irish fabrics and patterns and for a silhouette that wrapped rather than fitted the body. Laurel could have dressed no more unlike Fay (and the rest of the Mount Salus women) if she had wanted to.

Welty's technical finesse in her handling of symbol in *The Optimist's Daughter* seems to run aground, however, in her usage of Mardi Gras as the enveloping atmosphere of part 1. "It was a Monday morning of early March" when the novel begins (3). Anyone familiar with the carnival calendar would immediately know that Mardi Gras must be the following day, Tuesday; a Tuesday in early March is the latest possible date for Mardi Gras. And yet three weeks later the judge is still in the hospital recuperating from his eye operation and it is still carnival season (24, 31). As several critics have pointed out, "the unmistakable sound of hundreds, of thousands of people *blundering*" is an important symbolic reference point for all instances of ritualized human activity in the novel (43). Blundering is just what Laurel wants to avoid; poise in human relationships is her preference—and her weakness, as the crease in her skirt ably shows. Welty's apparent disregard for the actual calendar of pre-Lenten events underscores the literary importance of the motif of "people *blundering*." The error functions like a reversed palimpsest—something significant in the writer's design and intention that should have been "painted out" but was in fact left in the finished work.

The thematic importance of the "error" of leaving carnival in when it should have given way to Lent can be seen in the enhanced meaning it gives to the convocation of Dalzells. The judge shares a room with Mr. Dalzell, suffering terminal cancer and already dwelling mentally in the past. The hallucinations of Mr. Dalzell, besides providing local color and part of the construct of kin and community in the thematics of the novel, also translates as a warning against fetishizing the past and memory. In the father's (Mr. Dalzell's) memory, the son (Archie Lee) is still and always will be a child who cannot be entrusted with his own life. Mr. Dalzell seems to mistake the judge in the adjoining bed for his disappointing son, who cannot seem to follow the ritualized discipline of the hunt: father scolds son to keep his gun loaded and to keep the fire going (28, 29). While Mr. Dalzell hectors his absent son, Laurel tends to her unresponsive father. Structured parallels in scene communicate if the characters do not.

As Mr. Dalzell's illness draws inevitably to his death, his tribe congregates in the ward, keeping the kind of vigil that clearly, but covertly, embarrasses Laurel. Fay, on the other hand, is welcomed:

> There was an empty chair in the circle pulled up around a table, and Fay sat down among five or six grown men and women who all had the old woman's likeness. Their coats were on the table in a heap together, and open shoeboxes and paper sacks stood about on the floor; they were a family in the middle of their supper. (35)

The Dalzells might be sloppy in sumptuary manners, but like a true human hive, they "never let the conversation die" (36). Crudely but effectively the Dalzells "blunder" into solacing one another, even if they cannot sustain the physical life of their patriarch. They observe hierarchical rituals of visitation; by age and sex, members of the clan must go into the intensive care ward to visit the dying Mr. Dalzell. Archie Lee, exacting one last measure of revenge on his hectoring father, refuses to take his turn. If they can do nothing in reality to rescue the father from death, at least they talk the right talk:

> "If they don't give your dad no water by next time round, tell you what, we'll go in there all together and pour it down him," promised the old mother. "If he's going to die, I don't want him to die wanting water." (39)

The Dalzells as a body resolve "not to go gentle into that good night." Framed by the enveloping motif of blundering, the Dalzells's actions rise above local color and hillbilly comic relief. In the face of death (Mardi Gras is the day before Ash Wednesday, when many Christians remind themselves of death by daubing ashes on their foreheads), they loudly proclaim defiance.

Laurel, lacking metaphysical or tribal religion, reads literature to her father in a hushed voice. But the measured tones of Dickens being read (the judge's favorite is *Nicholas Nickleby*) cannot become the teeming life of actual Nicklebys and Crummellses. When Fay had "taken ahold" of her husband and tried to rouse him to life, she had attempted what the Dalzells were doing as a group (32). Laurel was appalled by the physicality of Fay's actions; but her rejection of Fay in the latter's blundering rescue attempt only reinforces the meaning of the wrinkle in her well-tailored suit: the fault line that runs through her character.

Part 2 of the novel takes place back home in Mount Salus, Mississippi, the county seat where Judge McKelva practiced law and where the McKelva family lived a masque of contentment. Nostalgia is the climate for this section of the novel, and from Laurel's outbursts it is clear that (to give Heilbrun her due) the communal nostalgia masks her personal anger. Welty again uses a ritualized human behavior, the funeral of a prominent man, to explore the instabilities in the formalized emotions and gestures that paper over the fact of death. This is a structure she had used in earlier work. "The Wanderers," the story that brings *The Golden Apples* to its culmination, is very similar in plot, pacing, range and depth of characterization, and theme.

When Laurel steps off the train carrying the judge's body home for burial, she steps into a living present that for her is a living past. If it is a cliché to say "you can't go home again," it is closer to the truth to say that if you do go, "home" is neither what it was nor what you need now. Laurel's progress through this deceptive terrain begins when she is greeted by the six bridesmaids who, by using her nickname, Polly, try to maneuver her back into the past. The undertaker, wryly named Mr. Pitts, approaches Laurel, since he recognizes her from the past arrangements for her mother, for instructions. Laurel has to suffer being overruled by Fay, who reminds all present that the past has given way to a new present: "'I'm Mrs. McKelva now'" (50).

The momentum of Mount Salus, which has never accepted Fay as Mrs. McKelva or as anything other than a kind of gold digger, proceeds to take over the funeral and the meanings of the life and death of its community leader. Fay puts up a fight from the outside, holding the trump card of title to the McKelva house and, therefore, to a "place" in Mount Salus society whether it wants her or not. Laurel puts up a fight from the out-side as well; she had chosen to live her life in Chicago. Still, vestigial Mount Salus reactions put her at odds with everyone. Laurel wants the coffin closed, but Fay's wishes for an open coffin carry, with the concurrence of many of the community who want a show (63). Major Bullock invites Fay's family to the funeral, following implicit instructions from the judge; Laurel feels muscled out of her own grief by their presence (101). Major Bullock also tells tall tales about Judge McKelva's exploits in the old days, embroidering in ways Laurel knows to be fictional (79–80). Whatever possessive intent Laurel might have harbored is thwarted; and the anger accumulates insider her.

With her father in his grave and Fay on her way back to Texas for a recuperative visit with kin she had earlier denied, Laurel is left alone in the Mount Salus house to come to terms with family myth and questions of her own past. It is in these scenes, where Laurel remembers her mother and images from the marriage of her parents preserved as well in memory, that the re-remembering in *One Writer's Beginnings* comes into play as a set of annotations to the novel.

Part 3 of the novel follows Laurel in the harrowing of her memory. Here, as the lines of the novel and the memoir over-lap, the two texts converge. Much of the judge's character can be seen in the sketch of Christian Welty in *One Writer's Begin-nings.* Both the fictional father and the real one valued ratio-nality and thought in terms of the future rather than the past. The writer's father cherished instruments and tools—a tele-scope, railway timetables, watches, ax and rope for escape from hotel rooms should a fire break out in the night. Clinton McKelva preserved his files on several flood control projects he had supervised for the county (119–20). Controlling the random current of events is the sign of both fathers.

Mothers are antitheses. In *The Optimist's Daughter* the writer represents this divergence in several ways. One of the most characteristic, because oblique and suggestive, is Welty's association of freely flowing water with Becky after the text has identified the judge as intent to channel and control unexpected floods. The remembered story of Becky's emergency trip with her father, Laurel's grandfather, from their home in the West Virginia mountains down the Elk River to a hospital in Baltimore where the father's acute appendicitis might be treated is apparently taken from Welty's mother's history. Accepting the challenge of circumstances rather than remolding them to a rational design seems to be the theme represented by current and flood in both texts. Laurel is stymied at an answer as to how any two human beings of such ingrained difference could ever live together, much less love one another. Her own marriage, lasting scarcely a year before her husband was killed in the Pacific in World War II, hardly qualifies Laurel as "married," and thus helps her very little in penetrating the riddle of her parents' marriage.

Remembering her parents' deep-seated cross-purposes, Laurel is torn between loyalty to mother or to father, or to the marriage as an entity in itself. Clearly, Becky's character in her lingering final illness leads Laurel to question the good sense of marriage at all. As she deteriorated, Becky became more irascible, less tolerant of those closest to her. Deep in her "torments" (148), Becky had seized upon the desire to visit her West Virginia home once more. Her condition was such that everyone knew such a trip to be impossible, yet her husband vowed to do it.

> "I'll carry you there, Becky."
> "Lucifer!" she cried. "*Liar!*"
> That was when he [the judge] started, of course, being what he scowlingly called an optimist. (150)

The memory clearly lodges with guilt in Laurel's mind; as the only offspring of this marriage, she is "responsible" for the coupling of two antithetical human beings whose relationship came to the point of one condemning the other.

Fay's presence is the trigger to the guilt, for she is the wife Laurel's father chooses to replace the one who called him a liar. From the early sections of *The Optimist's Daughter* through the burial of the judge and Fay's departure for Texas, Laurel and the other characters satisfy themselves that their antipathy to Fay originates in class difference. This was Cleanth Brooks's verdict: Fay has no class. Her clothes, contrasted to Laurel's, bear no designer labels and, hence, no style. Her taste in interior decoration of the Mount Salus house, contrasted in Laurel's memory to "the way it was," is tacky. The rough-and-ready manner of her speech ("You bet your boots," she tells Mr. Pitts when she has hammered him into agreement on the funeral [50]) contrasts with the measured hum of the bridesmaids. On all counts Fay is convicted of utter tackiness. She has soiled the sacred places with her nail polish (121–22) and desecrated the holy objects with profane use—Becky's breadboard (doubly sacred because it was made by Laurel's brief husband) used for shelling walnuts and marred by cigarette burns as if it were the surrogate victim of some twisted physical torture (172ff).

Laurel stores up days, weeks, and years of anger and frustration through these memories, and probably should thank Fay for waltzing back into the Mount Salus home unexpected at the last moment before her departure for Chicago. Mixed into Laurel's rage, however, are causes more personal than class rivalry.

There is an indication of the nature of Laurel's discomfort earlier in the novel. Soon after her father's eye operation, early in his ultimately futile recuperation, Laurel loses a contest for her father's favor:

> "Tell me something you would like to have," Laurel begged him. Fay, bending down over him, placed her lighted cigarette between his lips. His chest lifted visibly as he drew on it, and after a moment she took it away and his chest slowly fell as the smoke slowly traveled out of his mouth. She bent and gave it to him again.
>
> *"There's* something," she said.
>
> "Don't let the fire go out, son!" called Mr. Dalzell. (29)

With characteristic yet oblique economy, Welty suggests Laurel's lack and Fay's surplus: sexuality. Although Fay's tendering of the cigarette might seem like a kitschy scene from a 1940s B-movie, just as clearly it functions as a coded message from Fay to Laurel that the stepmother can give "something" to the judge that is beyond the daughter's power. This interpretation might even be extended to a claim that Fay's display of uninhibited sexual power exposes Laurel as shut off from similar connection not only by a common taboo but also by an essential withholding in her character. She recoils from Mardi Gras as too many people "blundering." For the long period of her father's hospital stay, Laurel maneuvers shifts at his bedside so that she and Fay "were hardly ever in the same place at the same time" (18). Even asleep, separated from Fay in a New Orleans rooming house only by "a landlord's strip of wallboard," Laurel is uncomfortable:

> Where there was no intimacy, Laurel shrank from contact; she shrank from that thin board and from the vague apprehension that some night she might hear Fay cry or laugh like a stranger at something she herself would rather not know. (18)

Keeping at bay what she "would rather not know" winds Laurel up like a compressed spring until the release in her encounter with Fay over the breadboard.

The intimacy claimed on Laurel's behalf in the passage quoted above, and the intimacy she fears and indirectly witnesses when Fay and her father share the cigarette, are not one and the same. The pressure to make them the same causes the tantalizing and powerful inconclusiveness of the ending of *The Optimist's Daughter,* an inconclusiveness that *One Writer's Beginnings* only partially redresses.

The gossip session involving Laurel, the bridesmaids, and Mrs. Pease the day after the burial of the judge (105–17) establishes the frame for the ending. While Laurel pulls weeds, her mother's voice and consciousness occupy her, and she hears the surrounding talk as her mother might have heard it. Although the women rate Fay beneath notice on her cooking and housekeeping skills, there is a subtext that clearly, if faintly, comes to the surface. Miss Tennyson Bullock observes that the house was often left in disarray; the minister's wife, Mrs. Bolt, completes the point from an information source that is not attributed, but is nevertheless on the inside: "'Their bed wasn't made'"(106). The implication is that the couple were using the bed for more than sleeping, but the gossipers evade the conclusion by changing the nature of the relationship, as they prefer to see it, from sex to dotage: "'Doted. You've hit on it. That's the word,' said Miss Tennyson" (107). Inserting a different word, however, will not alter the case in reality; the mockingbird who kibitzes from the dogwood tree pours out derisive commentary to that end (105). In fact, the ladies themselves seem to have difficulty in keeping to "doting" as the official line. When Miss Tennyson Bullock wonders aloud whether something had happened to the judge's "judgment," Mrs. Pease answers the partially asked question: "'He wasn't as old as all that,' agreed Mrs. Pease. "I'm older. By a trifle'" (107). "'A man can feel compunction for a child like Fay and still not have to carry it that far,' said Miss Tennyson" (107). "Compunction" is not so neat an evasion, and the mockingbird continues his derision.

What the ladies waltz around, and what Laurel hears with an inner ear, is that an unsocialized sexuality (the kind, for example, Welty had earlier embodied in Don McInnis in the story "Asphodel" or made the subject of farce in *The Ponder Heart*) might naturally exist in overt or covert tension with the value of physical moderation, personified next door to the McKelva house in Miss Adele Courtland with her patient waiting and her proper grammar: "'It's I,'" Miss Adele announces to Laurel the day of the wake (55). Laurel, through the harrowing of her memory, comes to understand that the marriage of her parents, Clinton McKelva and Becky Thurston, veiled just such a tension. Laurel cannot keep out of the mix of memory and anxiety the sexual power that the signifier "Fay" triggers: at one moment she fears that there might have been several "Fays" on her father's many business trips and that "Fay might already have been faithless to her father's memory" when she returns from her post-funeral excursion to Texas (179). Fay has burgeoned to mythic stature. A late, sharp memory of her own marriage to Philip Hand discloses a bitter truth to Laurel: her own marriage was too brief to stand as useful answer to "Fay" in all her range of meaning (154–55).

Much more than simple memory, then, is at stake when Fay clatters into the Mount Salus house on the morning Laurel returns to Chicago. Memories of her mother as member of the West Virginia family have reminded Laurel of her own resistance to the shock of uncontrolled intimacy. The memory of her grandmother's pigeons, eating from each other's craws, continues to shock Laurel—as the exchange of cigarettes between the judge and Fay had—with the surrender of physical integrity for the sake of saving intimacy (139–41). On one side are powerful characters who live in a world where the separating, privatizing membranes of self are naturally permeable in sex and soluble in death; on another side are those who fight to hold the line of self.

When Laurel seizes the breadboard, then, she seizes the token of the latter, the fiercely held faith that self is different in kind from other forms of existence, warranted by its own will against dissolution:

"My husband made it for my mother, so she'd have a good one. Phil had the gift—the gift of his hands. And he planed—fitted—glued—clamped—it's made on the true, look and see, it's still as straight as his T-square. Tongued and grooved, tight-fitted, every edge—" (175–76)

Memory, Laurel wants to insist, is the correlative to Phil's "gift of his hands," the craft or art that takes disparate pieces and clamps them into an integral, inviolate thing. As passionately as Laurel pushes this argument on Fay, Fay resists, and her resistance comes from a source perhaps more vulgar than Laurel's but no less passionate and powerful. As often as Laurel insists that the past has determined the meaning of ourselves and our things, Fay counters with an equally powerful argument: time moves on, oblivious to individual memory:

"She [Becky] made the best bread in Mount Salus."
"All right! Who cares? She's not making it now." (173)

As Fay proves equal to Laurel's attacks with memory, she also deflects accusations that she is merely her body, merely her sexuality. In these accusations Laurel seems to take her mother's part, implicitly, against the judge, her father:

"Fay, my mother knew you'd get into her house. She never needed to be told," said Laurel. "She predicted you."

"Predict? You *predict* the *weather,*" said Fay.

You *are* the weather, thought Laurel. And the weather to come: there'll be many a one more like you, in this life. (173)

Compared with Edna Earle Ponder's rueful comment about the Peacocks ("They're not dying out"), Laurel's unspoken response to Fay is bitter. Now that both of her parents are dead, what can it matter to her how many more Fays there might be? It can matter if it is not just the memory of her mother and father that troubles Laurel, but her attitude toward the course she has given to her own life: a brief marriage to an ideal man who did not live long enough to confess his reality, decades of what kind of emotional and physical celibacy away from Mount Salus. A parting shot, like the rejoinder to Fay about the weather kept wordless except in Laurel's mind, underscores her anxiety. To Laurel, Fay represents something deeper than rampant vulgarity; she is the life from which Laurel has shied away, a way she will never be, the answer to a question Laurel has been too careful to ask.

Since *One Writer's Beginnings* overlaps *The Optimist's Daughter* so closely it is impossible not to read the later text back upon the earlier. Becky's hold upon Laurel is described in Mrs. Welty's hold on her daughter and the rest of the children. "Control" and "guilt" are the watchwords, no different in Welty's case than for any child anywhere. There *is* anger in *One Writer's Beginnings,* just as there is anger in the character of Laurel. In the latter text it is mixed with sadness—sadness for moments of connection and possibility lost. One such lost moment, Welty remembers, was the daughter's inevitable question to her mother about the origin of babies.

> On the night we came the closest to having it over with, she started to tell me without being asked, and I ruined it by yelling, "Mother, look at the lightning bugs!" (16)

A kind of bonding that might have taken place, easing mother and daughter into the scheme of the world and of each other, is delayed or denied. Welty's previous autobiographical fiction ("The Winds" and "June Recital") had hinted all along that close to the heart of her vision is the failed or denied or simply missed mother-daughter exchange.

Welty learned the facts of life and daughterhood another way, a way encoded with guilt—no one's fault. Rummaging in her mother's bureau drawers, the child found a cache of memory: a braid of hair and, on a later foray, "two polished buffalo nickels" (16–17). The child wanted to spend the windfall, but got only unexpected passion from her mother. The coins had been used to cover the eyes of a baby, born before Eudora Welty, who had died. "The future story writer in the child I was must have taken unconscious note and stored it away then: one secret is liable to be revealed in the place of another that is harder to tell, and the substitute secret when nakedly exposed is often the more appalling" (17). When Laurel goes looking for the secret of her parents' love, she finds a "substitute secret," the friction of two people in an intimate place.

As much as Laurel, in the denouement to *The Optimist's Daughter,* tries to keep her mother in the privileged place, the "unconscious note" sounds. Becky's "strength" had been as often a pain to those around her as it was a bulwark. The writer's mother had inflicted guilt upon her daughter in the name of concern and had sought to control the family's life in the name of kindness:

> Even as we grew up, my mother could not help imposing herself between her children and whatever it was they might take it in mind to reach out for in the world. For she would get it for them, if it was good enough for them—she would have to be very sure—and give it to them, at whatever cost to herself: valiance was in her very fiber. She stood always prepared in herself to challenge the world in our place. She did indeed tend to make the world look dangerous, and so it had been to her. A way had to be found around her love sometimes, without challenging *that,* and at the same time cherishing it in its unassailable strength. (39)

The mother had made sure, in ways only a parent can, that the child's joy was framed in guilt. Giving her daughter the pleasure of seeing a play meant that the daughter could never afterward "bear my pleasure for my guilt" (19).

As the mother-daughter bond imagined in *The Optimist's Daughter* is so identifiable with the one remembered in *One Writer's Beginnings,* it is impossible to read the one without the other. Laurel's "transcendence" in the conclusion to the novel is as much flight from the scene as release, all debts paid. She has not so much "solved the problem" of Fay as simply turned her back on it. And, since Fay is the future and the future is life, Laurel's "triumph" might be in name only.

One Writer's Beginnings, published a dozen years after *The Optimist's Daughter,* provides a kind of continuation and extension of the lines charted but left inconclusive in the novel. The memoir's powerful attractiveness to readers, and Welty's stated theme in writing it, surge from the tension explored in competing characters in the earlier novel: the tension between daring and shelter. The last sentences of *One Writer's Beginnings* seal the theme:

> As you have seen, I am a writer who came of a sheltered life. A sheltered life can be a daring life as well. For all serious daring starts from within. (104)

Laurel, set within these terms, has imposed limits on her daring. Fay, perhaps too recklessly, has abolished limits; maybe she could not afford them in the first place. Welty, the writer who imagined them both, explores limits, daring, and the circumstances under which she has known both.

As Becky is the enigmatic, charged figure in *The Optimist's Daughter,* Welty's mother, Chestina Andrews Welty, is the magnet in *One Writer's Beginnings.* Welty treats the reltionship between her mother's character and the writer's limits gingerly; it is clear, however, that the mother-daughter relationship shaped the writer, and the woman, profoundly.

Mrs. Welty's power over the family was wielded through guilt and control. In the first of the three lectures that make up *One Writer's Beginnings,* "Listening," the otherwise idyllic Welty household is riven with Mrs. Welty's manipulation of guilty feelings:

> When my mother would tell me that she wanted me to have something because she as a child had never had it, I wanted, or I partly wanted, to give it back. All my life I continued to feel that bliss for me would have to imply my mother's deprivation or sacrifice. I don't think it would have occurred to her what a double emotion I felt, and indeed I know that it was being unfair to her, for what she said was simply the truth. (19)

The anecdote that follows is clearly instructive. There are two tickets to a show, and Mrs. Welty gives hers to her daughter:

> In the Century first-row balcony, where their seats always were, I'd be sitting beside my father at this hour beyond my bedtime carried totally away by the performance, and then suddenly the thought of my mother staying home with my sleeping younger brothers, missing the spectacle at this moment before my eyes, and doing without all the excitement and wonder that filled my being, would arrest me and I could hardly bear my pleasure for my guilt. (19)

The feeling is not rare; many children manage to become convinced that all they feel as pleasure comes at the expense of their parents. Welty makes the feeling the cornerstone of her self-consciousness as a writer. "I have never managed to handle the guilt. In the act and the course of writing stories, these are two of the springs, one bright, one dark, that feed the stream" (20).

Mrs. Welty, the intensely spun hub of the family, comes through again as the writer remembers her adolescence. "As an adolescent I was a slammer of drawers and a packer of suitcases. I was responsible for scenes." Control was the mother's commandment and the lesson of her life: "'I don't understand where you children *get* it,' said my mother. 'I never lose my temper. I just get hurt.' (But that was it.)" (38).

Showing "hurt" is a dependable mechanism of control, and one that defuses retaliation. Becky, in *The Optimist's Daughter,* manipulates her husband and daughter using a similar strategy, especially in the final stages of her illness, when she accuses them both of failing to cure her (151). In the novel Becky's intensity is dramatized as poetic vision; when she excoriates the minister, Dr. Bolt, for his failure to grasp the meaning of the mythic white strawberries, Becky is a seer in the most basic sense (149).

The mother of the memoir, however, is drawn more complexly into the mother-daughter relationship of the novel by her failure to tell what she has seen of childbirth and sex. The parent's clumsiness, and often utter failure, in telling the next generation the story of how they got here is a comic staple—probably because failure to know the right facts at the right time can result in embarrassment or worse. Welty treats her experience as her mother's pain, not her own (15–18).

Starting the scene with familiar parental hemming and hawing, Welty ends it by blaming herself for bringing up the painful memory of a baby brother who died soon after birth, a birth that left her mother with septicemia that nearly took her life:

> Now, her hair [which had been cut off during her illness and kept] was long again, it would reach in a braid down her back, and now I was her child. She hadn't died. And when I came, I hadn't died either. Would she ever? Would I ever? I couldn't face *ever*. I must have rushed into her lap, demanding her like a baby. And she had put her first-born aside again, for me. (18)

There is no way to assess accurately the impact of the conflation of the request for one's story of origin and the "response" of death for the firstborn and the mother's miraculous survival. Nevertheless, Welty places the two incidents in narrative dependency; the one elicits the other. And this narrative produces another conclusion crucial in opening *The Optimist's Daughter*'s secreted meanings:

> I have always been shy physically. This in part tended to keep me from rushing into things, including relationships, headlong. Not rushing headlong, though I may have wanted to, but beginning to write stories about people, I drew near slowly; noting and guessing, apprehending, hoping, drawing my eventual conclusions out of my own heart, I *did* venture closer to where I wanted to go. As time and my imagination led me on, I did plunge. (22)

Laurel, however, does not seem to have "plunged." Even in her marriage to Philip Hand, Laurel cannot remember "a single blunder in their short life together" (162). Given the accumulated meaning of *blunder* in the novel, and the intertextual impact of the memoir, Laurel's cherished memory of husband and marriage seems at least as plausibly an unconscious admission of failure as a celebration of the "plunge" into intimacy.

Intertextual connections and conversations between *The Optimist's Daughter* and *One Writer's Beginnings* occur on several levels. Welty's loving sketch of her father lends color and resonance to the character of Clinton McKelva, and vice versa, though the one is not a key to the other. Her fuller treatment of her mother and her mother's family in West Virginia results in more prickly correspondence. Chestina Andrews Welty and Becky Thurston McKelva are both present to their respective daughters as women whose lives were laid down for daughters who, in their turn, were held accountable for restitution in their own lives.

The mother's presence is felt right up to the conclusion of *One Writer's Beginnings,* and radiates as if in a prismatic presence through all of Welty's work as she reconsiders it from the critic's post outside the work:

> What I have put into her [the character of Miss Eckhart in "June Recital"] is my passion for my own life work, my own art. Exposing yourself to risk is a truth Miss Eckhart and I had in common. What animates and possesses me is what drives Miss Eckhart, the love of her art and the love of giving it, the desire to give it until there

is no more left. Even in the small and literal way, what I had done in assembling and connecting all the stories in *The Golden Apples,* and bringing them off as one, was not too unlike the June recital itself.

Not in Miss Eckhart as she stands solidly and almost opaquely in the surround of her story, but in the making of her character out of my most inward and most deeply feeling self, I would say I have found my voice in my fiction.

Of course any writer is in part all of his characters. How otherwise would they be known to him, occur to him, become what they are? I was also part Cassie in that same story, the girl who hung back, and indeed part of most of the main characters in the connected stories into whose minds I go. Except for Virgie, the heroine. She is right outside me. She is powerfully like Miss Eckhart, her co-equal in stubborn and passionate feeling, while more expressive of it—but fully apart from me. (101)

Writers sometimes make the best critics of their own work not for what they say, but for what they try not to say and pretend not to know or remember. Miss Eckhart and Virgie stand in eloquent relationship with Laurel and her mother, and with the writer and the mother of Welty's memoir. What Welty professes not to remember about Miss Eckhart is that to become the possessor of her own passion she must strike her mother dumb (*GA* 54–55). And Virgie, who stands as daughter to Miss Eckhart as much as she does to Katie Rainey, her biological mother, must sever the cords of control (symbolized in the metronome) and take the risks of the daring life of the artist.

Not surprisingly, Welty supplies a kind of coda to her career in the last two books she has published. Extending and confirming patterns ventured in earlier works, *The Optimist's Daughter* and *One Writer's Beginnings* set the family as the crucial dramatic situation, and the mother-daughter relation as the power source for the author's plots, themes, and patterns of imagery and symbol. That the author continually opens and closes the patterns, as she does with *The Optimist's Daughter* and *One Writer's Beginnings,* strongly suggests where readers should begin to look in understanding Eudora Welty and her fiction.

Chapter 1: *A Curtain of Green and Other Stories*

1. Henry Seidel Canby, "The School of Cruelty," review of *Sanctuary* by William Faulkner, *Saturday Review,* 21 March 1931, 673–74.

2. Sarah Schiff, "Stories Too Green To Burn," review of *A Curtain of Green* by Eudora Welty, *Springfield (Massachusetts) Republican,* 11 January 1942, 7e.

3. Eudora Welty to Ford Madox Ford, 27 October 1938, Welty Collection, Mississippi Department of Archives and History. Used with permission.

Chapter 2: *The Robber Bridegroom*

1. L. S. Munn, review of *The Robber Bridegroom* by Eudora Welty, *Springfield (Massachusetts) Republican,* 22 November 1942, 7e.

2. Orville Prescott, "A Handful of Rising Stars." *New York Times Book Review,* 21 March 1943, 13.

3. *Mississippi: The WPA Guide to the Magnolia State* (1938; rpt. Jackson: University Press of Mississippi, 1988).

Chapter 3: *The Wide Net and Other Stories*

1. Eudora Welty to Diarmuid Russell, 18 January 1941; in Michael Kreyling, *Author and Agent: Eudora Welty and Diarmuid Russell* (New York: Farrar Straus and Giroux, 1990), 58.

2. Kreyling, *Author and Agent,* 58.

3. "Sense and Sensibility," review of *The Wide Net* by Eudora Welty, *Time,* 27 September 1943, 100.

4. "Briefly Noted," review of *The Wide Net* by Eudora Welty, *New Yorker,* 25 September 1943, 80.

5. Welty to Russell, n.d. [late May/early June 1941]; Kreyling, *Author and Agent,* 74.

6. Kreyling, *Author and Agent,* 68–71.

7. *Kenyon Review* 6 (September 1944): 246–59. Reprinted in Harold Bloom, ed., *Modern Critical Views: Eudora Welty* (New York: Chelsea House, 1986), 19–28.

8. Kreyling, *Author and Agent,* 84.

9. Kreyling, *Author and Agent,* 67.

10. Harriet Pollack, "On Welty's Use of Allusion: Expectations and Their Revision in 'The Wide Net,' *The Robber Bridegroom,* and 'At the Landing,'" *The Southern Quarterly* 29.1 (Fall 1990): 5–31.

11. Kreyling, *Author and Agent,* 92.

12. Laurie Champion, ed., *The Critical Response to Eudora Welty's Fiction* (Westport, Conn.: Greenwood Press, 1994), 328.

Chapter 4: *Delta Wedding*

1. Hamilton Basso, "Look Away, Look Away," review of *Delta Wedding, The New Yorker,* 3 September 1946, 56. Reprinted in Champion, *Critical Response,* 106–7.

2. See "The Art of Fiction XLVII: Eudora Welty" [An interview by Linda Kuehl], in *Conversations with Eudora Welty,* edited by Peggy W. Prenshaw (Jackson: University Press of Mississippi, 1984), 75.

3. "Fiction in Review," in Champion, *Critical Response,* 105.

4. Isaac Rosenfeld, "Double Standard," review of *Delta Wedding, New Republic,* 29 April 1946, 633–34; Harnett T. Kane, "Eudora

Welty's Authentic and Vital Talent," review of *Delta Wedding, New York Herald Tribune Weekly Book Review,* 14 April 1946, 3.

5. Albert J. Devlin, *Eudora Welty's Chronicle: A Story of Mississippi Life* (Jackson: University Press of Mississippi, 1983).

6. See also Lehman Engel, *This Bright Day* (New York: Macmillan, 1974), 41.

7. Louise Westling, *Sacred Groves and Ravaged Gardens: The Fiction of Eudora Welty, Carson McCullers, and Flannery O'Connor* (Athens: University of Georgia Press, 1985).

Chapter 5: *The Golden Apples*

1. Hamilton Basso, "Morgana, Mississippi," review of *The Golden Apples, The New Yorker,* 3 September 1949, 63–64; Malcolm Cowley, review of *The Golden Apples, New York Post,* 1 September 1949; Francis Steegmuller, "Small-Town Life," review of *The Golden Apples, New York Times Book Review,* 21 August 1949, 5.

2. Coleman Rosenberger, "Miss Welty's Trance-like Mississippi," review of *The Golden Apples, New York Herald Tribune Books,* 21 August 1949, 6.

3. Olive Dean Hormel, "Tales Minus Vision," review of *The Golden Apples, Christian Science Monitor,* 24 August 1949, 16.

4. Peggy W. Prenshaw, ed., *Conversations with Eudora Welty* (Jackson: University Press of Mississippi, 1984), 224.

5. William Faulkner, *Light in August* (New York: Harrison Smith and Robert Haas, 1932), 145–46.

6. Patricia S. Yaeger, "'Because a Fire Was in My Head': Eudora Welty and Dialogic Imagination," in *Welty: A Life in Literature,* edited by Albert J. Devlin (Jackson: University Press of Mississippi, 1988), 146.

Chapter 6: *The Ponder Heart*

1. Louis D. Rubin Jr., review of *The Ponder Heart* by Eudora Welty, *Baltimore Sun,* 12 January 1954.

2. Charles Poore, "Books of the Times," review of *The Ponder Heart* by Eudora Welty, *New York Times,* 7 January 1954, 29.

3. V. S. Pritchett, "Bossy Edna Earle Had a Word for Everything," *New York Times Book Review,* 10 January 1954, 5.

4. Harrison Smith, "Welty Novel Happy One," *Roanoke Times,* 10 January 1954. This review, or edited versions of it, appeared in several U.S. daily newspapers.

5. Ruth Vande Kieft, *Eudora Welty,* rev. ed. (Boston: G. K. Hall, 1986), 56.

6. Robert B. Holland, "Dialogue As a Reflection of Place in *The Ponder Heart,*" *American Literature* 35 (November 1963): 357.

7. Alfred Appel Jr., *A Season of Dreams: The Fiction of Eudora Welty* (Baton Rouge: Louisiana State University Press, 1965), 57.

8. Peter Schmidt, *The Heart of the Story: Eudora Welty's Short Fiction* (Jackson: University Press of Mississippi, 1991).

Chapter 7: *The Bride of the* Innisfallen

1. John K. Hutchens, "Miss Welty's Somewhat Puzzling Art," *New York Herald Tribune Books,* 10 April 1955, 2.

2. Sterling North, review of *The Bride of the* Innisfallen, *New York World Telegram & Sun,* 7 April 1955, 22.

3. William Peden, "The Incomparable Welty," *Saturday Review,* 9 April 1955, 18.

4. Ruth M. Vande Kieft, *Eudora Welty,* rev. ed. (Boston: G. K. Hall, 1986), 126. In the first edition, this sentence appears on pages 150–51.

5. Alfred Appel Jr., *A Season of Dream: The Fiction of Eudora Welty* (Baton Rouge: Louisiana State University Press, 1965), 242–43.

6. Michael Kreyling, *Eudora Welty's Achievement of Order* (Baton Rouge: Louisiana State University Press, 1980).

7. Noel Polk, "Water, Wanderers, and Weddings: Love in Eudora Welty," in *Eudora Welty: A Form of Thanks,* edited by Ann J. Abadie and Louis J. Dollarhide (Jackson: University Press of Mississippi, 1979), 104–10; "Going to Naples and Other Places in Eudora Welty's Fiction," in *Eudora Welty: Eye of the Storyteller,* edited by Dawn Trouard (Kent, Ohio: Kent State University Press, 1989), 153–64.

8. Ruth D. Weston, *Gothic Traditions and Narrative Techniques in the Fiction of Eudora Welty* (Baton Rouge: Louisiana State University Press, 1994).

9. See Vande Kieft, *Eudora Welty,* ch. 7.

10. Eudora Welty, "Writing and Analyzing a Story," in *The Eye of the Story: Selected Essays & Reviews* (New York: Random House, 1977), 108.

11. Dawn Trouard, "Welty's Anti-Ode to a Nightingale: Gabriella's Southern Passage," *Mississippi Quarterly* 50 (fall 1997): 669–88.

Chapter 8: *Losing Battles*

1. Louis D. Rubin Jr., "Everything Brought Out in the Open: Eudora Welty's *Losing Battles,*" *Hollins Critic* 7.3 (1970): 1.

2. James Boatwright, review of *Losing Battles, New York Times Book Review,* 12 April 1970, 1.

3. Reynolds Price, "Frightening Gift," *Washington Post,* 17 April 1970, sec. C, p. 1,4.

4. Jonathan Yardley, "The Last Good One?" *New Republic,* 9 May 1970, 36.

5. Joyce Carol Oates, "Eudora's Web," *Atlantic Monthly,* April 1970, 120.

6. John W. Aldridge, "Eudora Welty: Metamorphosis of a Southern Lady Writer," *Saturday Review,* 11 April 1970, 21–23, 35–36.

Chapter 9: *The Optimist's Daughter* and *One Writer's Beginnings*

1. Cleanth Brooks, "The Past Reexamined: *The Optimist's Daughter,*" in *The Critical Response to Eudora Welty's Fiction,* edited by Laurie Champion (Westport, Conn.: Greenwood Press, 1994), 227.

2. Champion, *Critical Response,* 234.

3. Reynolds Price, "The Onlooker, Smiling: An Early Reading of *The Optimist's Daughter,*" in *A Common Room: Essays 1954–1987* (New York: Atheneum, 1987), 67.

4. Carolyn G. Heilbrun, *Writing a Woman's Life* (New York: W. W. Norton, 1988), 11.

Works by Eudora Welty

Books

A Curtain of Green and Other Stories. Garden City, N.Y.: Doubleday, Doran and Co., 1941; London: John Lane The Bodley Head, 1943.

The Robber Bridegroom. Garden City, N.Y.: Doubleday, Doran and Co., 1942; London: John Lane The Bodley Head, 1944.

The Wide Net and Other Stories. New York: Harcourt, Brace and Co., 1943; London: John Lane The Bodley Head, 1945.

Delta Wedding. New York: Harcourt, Brace and Co., 1946; London: The Bodley Head, 1947.

The Golden Apples. New York: Harcourt, Brace and Co., 1949; London: The Bodley Head, 1950.

The Ponder Heart. New York: Harcourt, Brace and Co., 1954; London: Hamish Hamilton, 1954.

The Bride of the Innisfallen *and Other Stories.* Harcourt, Brace and Co., 1955; London: Hamish Hamilton, 1955.

The Shoe Bird. New York: Harcourt, Brace & World, 1964.

Losing Battles. New York: Random House, 1970; London: Virago, 1982.

One Time, One Place: Mississippi in the Depression / A Snapshot Album. New York: Random House, 1971.

The Optimist's Daughter. New York: Random House, 1972; London: Andre Deutsch, 1973.

The Eye of the Story: Selected Essays and Reviews. New York: Random House, 1978; London: Virago, 1987.

The Collected Stories of Eudora Welty. New York: Harcourt Brace Jovanovich, 1980; London: Marion Boyars, 1981.

BIBLIOGRAPHY

One Writer's Beginnings. Cambridge: Harvard University Press, 1984; London: Faber and Faber, 1985.

Eudora Welty Photographs. Jackson: University Press of Mississippi, 1989.

Eudora Welty: Stories, Essays, & Memoir. New York: The Library of America, 1998.

Eudora Welty: Complete Novels. New York: The Library of America, 1998.

Uncollected Short Stories

"The Doll." *The Tanager* (Grinnell College, Grinnell, Iowa) 11 (June 1936): 11–14.

"Magic." *Manuscript* 3 (September–October 1936): 3–7.

"Retreat." *River: A Magazine of the Deep South* 1 (March 1937): 10–12.

"A Sketching Trip." *Atlantic Monthly* 175 (June 1945): 62–70.

"Hello and Good-Bye." *Atlantic Monthly* 180 (July 1947): 37–40.

Recordings

Eudora Welty Reading from Her Works: "Why I Live at the P.O.," "A Memory," and "A Worn Path." Caedmon Records TC-1010-A, 1952. Reissued on audiocassette as Caedmon Cassette CDL 51010, 1986.

On Story Telling. Columbia, Mo.: Audio Forum, 1961. Contains an early version of "Words into Fiction" and parts of "Writing and Analyzing a Story."

Eudora Welty Reads Her Stories: "Powerhouse" and "Petrified Man." Caedmon Records TC-1626, 1979; Caedmon Cassette CDL 51626.

The Optimist's Daughter. New York: Random House Audio-Books, 1986.

Selected Critical Works about Eudora Welty

Bibliographies

McHaney, Pearl Amelia. "A Eudora Welty Checklist, 1973–1986." In *Welty: A Life in Literature,* edited by Albert J. Devlin, 266–302. Jackson: University Press of Mississippi, 1988.

Polk, Noel. "A Eudora Welty Checklist, 1936–1972." In *Welty: A Life in Literature,* edited by Albert J. Devlin, 238–65. Jackson: University Press of Mississippi, 1988.

———. *Eudora Welty: A Bibliography of Her Work.* Jackson: University Press of Mississippi, 1994. Indispensable.

Swearingen, Bethany C. *Eudora Welty: A Critical Bibliography, 1936–1958.* Jackson: University Press of Mississippi, 1984.

Thompson, Victor H. *Eudora Welty: A Reference Guide.* Boston: G. K. Hall, 1976.

Essays and Reviews

Aldridge, John W. "Eudora Welty: Metamorphosis of a Southern Lady Writer." *Saturday Review,* 11 April 1970, 21–23, 35–36.

Atkinson, Brooks. Review of *The Ponder Heart* (stage adaptation). *New York Times,* 17 February 1956, 14:2.

Basso, Hamilton. "Look Away, Look Away, Look Away." Review of *Delta Wedding. New Yorker,* 11 May 1946, 89.

———. "Morgana, Mississippi." Review of *The Golden Apples. New Yorker,* 3 September 1949, 56.

Boatwright, James. "The Continuity of Love." *New Republic,* 10 June 1972, 24–25.

———. Review of *Losing Battles. New York Times Book Review,* 12 April 1970, 1, 32–34.

BIBLIOGRAPHY

"Briefly Noted." Review of *The Wide Net. New Yorker,* 25 September 1943, 80.

Cowley, Malcolm. "Seven New Stories by Eudora Welty." Review of *The Golden Apples. New York Post,* 1 September 1949.

Derleth, August. Review of *A Curtain of Green. Madison (Wisconsin)Times,* 7 December 1941.

Holland, Robert B. "Dialogue as a Reflection of Place in *The Ponder Heart.*" *American Literature* 35 (1963): 352–58.

Hormel, Olive Dean. "Talent Minus Vision." Review of *The Golden Apples. Christian Science Monitor,* 24 August 1949, 16.

Hutchens, John K. "Miss Welty's Somewhat Puzzling Art." *New York Herald Tribune Book Review,* 10 April 1955, 2.

Jackson, Joseph Henry. "Bookman's Notebook: Don't Miss Uncle Daniel Ponder." *San Francisco Chronicle,* 19 January 1954, 15.

Lehmann-Haupt, Christopher. "Books of the Times." Review of *Losing Battles. New York Times,* 10 April 1970, 37.

McHaney, Thomas L. "Eudora Welty and the Multitudinous Golden Apples." *Mississippi Quarterly* 26 (Fall 1973): 589–624.

Munn, L.. S. Review of *The Robber Bridegroom. Springfield (Massachusetts) Republican,* 22 November 1942, 7e.

North, Sterling. "Sterling North Reviews the Books." *New York World Telegram,* 7 April 1955.

Oates, Joyce Carol. "Eudora's Web." *Atlantic Monthly,* April 1970, 118–20, 122.

Peden, William. "The Incomparable Welty." *Saturday Review,* 9 April 1955, 18.

———. "A Trial with No Verdict." Review of *The Ponder Heart. Saturday Review,* 16 January 1954, 14.

Pollack, Harriet. "On Welty's Use of Allusion: Expectations and Their Revision in "The Wide Net," *The Robber Bridegroom,* and "At the Landing." *The Southern Quarterly* 29.1 (Fall 1990): 5–31. Reprinted in *Champion.*

BIBLIOGRAPHY

Poore, Charles. "Books of the Times." Review of *The Ponder Heart. New York Times,* 7 January 1954, 29.

Prescott, Orville. "A Handful of Rising Stars." *New York Times Book Review,* 21 March 1943, 13.

Price, Reynolds. "Frightening Gift." Review of *Losing Battles. Washington Post,* 17 April 1970, sec. C, p. 1, 4.

Pritchett, V. S. "Bossy Edna Earle Had a Word for Everything." *New York Times Book Review,* 10 January 1954, 5.

Rosenberger, Coleman. "Eudora Welty Tells a Wise and Comic Story of a Mississippi Town." Review of *The Ponder Heart. New York Herald Tribune Book Review,* 10 January 1954, 1.

———. "Miss Welty's Trance-like Mississippi." Review of *The Golden Apples. New York Herald Tribune Books,* 21 August 1949, 6.

Rubin, Louis D., Jr. "Everything Brought Out in the Open: Eudora Welty's Losing Battles." *Hollins Critic* 7.3 (1970): 1–7, 9–12.

Schiff, Sarah. "Stories Too Green to Burn." Review of *A Curtain of Green. Springfield (Massachusetts) Republican,* 11 January 1942, 7e.

"Sense and Sensibility." Review of *The Wide Net. Time,* 27 September 1943, 100–101.

Smith, Harrison. "Welty Novel Happy One." *Roanoke Times,* 10 January 1954.

Steegmuller, Francis. "Small-Town Life." Review of *The Golden Apples. New York Times Book Review,* 21 August 1949, 5.

Trouard, Dawn. "Diverting Swine: The Magical Relevancies of Eudora Welty's Ruby Fisher and Circe." In *The Critical Response to Eudora Welty's Fiction,* edited by Laurie Champion, 335–56. Westport, Conn.: Greenwood Press, 1994.

———. "Welty's Anti-Ode to a Nightingale: Gabriella's Southern Passage." *Mississippi Quarterly* 50 (Fall 1997): 669–88.

Warren, Robert Penn. "The Love and Separateness in Miss Welty." *Kenyon Review* 6 (1944): 246–59. Rev. version reprinted in Bloom, *Modern Critical Views: Eudora Welty,* 19–28.

BIBLIOGRAPHY

Yaeger, Patricia S. "'Because a Fire Was in My Head': Eudora Welty and the Dialogic Imagination." In *Welty: A Life in Literature,* edited by Albert J. Devlin, 139–67. Jackson: University Press of Mississippi, 1988.

Yardley, Jonathan. "The Last Good One?" *New Republic,* 9 May 1970, 33–36.

Books and Chapters

Appel, Alfred, Jr. *A Season of Dreams: The Fiction of Eudora Welty.* Baton Rouge: Louisiana State University Press, 1965.

Binding, Paul. *The Still Moment: Eudora Welty, Portrait of a Writer.* London: Virago, 1994.

Bloom, Harold, ed. *Modern Critical Views: Eudora Welty.* New York: Chelsea House Publishers, 1986. Contains essays by Robert Penn Warren and Reynolds Price mentioned in the text.

Carson, Barbara Harrell. *Eudora Welty: Two Pictures at Once in Her Frame.* Troy, N.Y.: Whitson, 1992.

Champion, Laurie, ed. *The Critical Response to Eudora Welty's Fiction.* Westport, Conn.: Greenwood Press, 1994. Contains important and representative reviews of Welty's books mentioned in the text, as well as samplings of new critical departures.

Devlin, Albert J. *Eudora Welty's Chronicle: A Story of Mississippi Life.* Jackson: University Press of Mississippi, 1983.

————, ed. *Welty: A Life in Literature.* Jackson: University Press of Mississippi, 1988. Contains the essay by Patricia Yaeger mentioned in the text, as well as important critical essays by Prenshaw, Pitavy-Souques, and others, and Pearl McHaney's update of Noel Polk's 1973 checklist.

Dollarhide, Louis, and Ann J. Abadie, eds. *Eudora Welty: A Form of Thanks.* Jackson: University Press of Mississippi, 1979.

BIBLIOGRAPHY

Engel, Lehman. *This Bright Day: An Autobiography.* New York: Macmillan, 1974. Chatty autobiography that contains some interesting anecdotes of Engel's Jackson escapades with Welty and other friends.

Evans, Elizabeth. *Eudora Welty.* New York: Ungar, 1981.

Gretlund, Jan Nordby. *Eudora Welty's Aesthetics of Place.* Odense, Denmark: Odense University Press, 1994. Densely argued interpretation of Welty as southern writer influenced by place and history.

Harrison, Suzan. *Eudora Welty and Virginia Woolf: Gender, Genre, and Influence.* Baton Rouge: Louisiana State University Press, 1997. Exploration of the "influence" of Woolf and feminist insights into Welty's fiction.

Heilbrun, Carolyn G. *Hamlet's Mother and Other Women.* New York: Columbia University Press, 1990. Critical essays exploring the vintage and kinds of feminist consciousness that shaped Welty and the writers she identified as powerful influences on her work.

———. *Writing a Woman's Life.* New York: W. W. Norton, 1988.

Kreyling, Michael. *Author and Agent: Eudora Welty and Diarmuid Russell.* New York: Farrar Straus & Giroux, 1991. Based on record of correspondence between Welty and her literary agent, this book traces the ups and downs of Welty's publishing career, her critical reputation, and the evolution of craft and vision.

———. *Eudora Welty's Achievement of Order.* Baton Rouge: Louisiana State University Press, 1980. A formalist literary study of major images, themes, and verbal patterns in Welty's work.

McHaney, Pearl Amelia, ed. *The Writer's Eye: Collected Book Reviews of Eudora Welty.* Jackson: University Press of Mississippi, 1994. Find Welty's review of Virginia Woolf, mentioned in chapter 4, here.

Manning, Carol S. *With Ears Opening Like Morning Glories: Eudora Welty and the Love of Storytelling.* Westport, Conn.: Greenwood

Press, 1985. A critical study that investigates forms of narrative in Welty's works.

Mark, Rebecca. *The Dragon's Blood: Feminist Intertextuality in Eudora Welty's* The Golden Apples. Jackson: University Press of Mississippi, 1994. An important book-length study of *The Golden Apples* indicating the new directions provided by feminist literary theory.

Marrs, Suzanne. *The Welty Collection: A Guide to the Eudora Welty Manuscripts and Documents at the Mississippi Department of Archive and History.* Jackson: University Press of Mississippi, 1988. Invaluable as a study of the multifarious aspects of Welty's creativity: manuscripts showing stages of revision, a history of Welty as photographer, a calendar of correspondence in the major archive of Welty materials.

Mortimer, Gail L. *Daughter of the Swan: Love and Knowledge in Eudora Welty's Fiction.* Athens: University of Georgia Press, 1994.

Prenshaw, Peggy Whitman, ed. *Conversations with Eudora Welty.* Jackson: University Press of Mississippi, 1984.

———, ed. *Eudora Welty: Critical Essays.* Jackson: University Press of Mississippi, 1979. An excellent collection of several essays covering the whole of Welty's career, her nonfiction and photography as well as fiction, by a full range of critics suggesting the differences in generational, gender, and theoretical outlook.

Price, Reynolds. *A Common Room: Essays 1954–1987.* New York: Atheneum, 1987. Contains his essay on *The Optimist's Daughter,* "The Onlooker, Smiling."

Randisi, Jennifer Lynn. *A Tissue of Lies: Eudora Welty and the Southern Romance.* Washington, D.C.: University Press of America, 1982.

Schmidt, Peter. *The Heart of the Story: Eudora Welty's Short Fiction.* Jackson: University Press of Mississippi, 1991. Important critical attempt to see all of Welty's short fiction within a single critical frame: the American woman writer and her literary traditions.

Trouard, Dawn, ed. *Eudora Welty: Eye of the Storyteller.* Kent, Ohio: Kent State University Press, 1989.

Turner, W. Craig, and Lee Emling Harding, eds. *Critical Essays on Eudora Welty.* Boston: G. K. Hall, 1989.

Vande Kieft, Ruth M. *Eudora Welty: Revised Edition.* Boston: G. K. Hall, 1986. Unless otherwise indicated, all references to Vande Kieft are taken from the revised edition, not the first edition (1962). The first edition was the first book-length study of Welty's fiction; updated in 1986 to include subsequently published works.

Westling, Louise. *Sacred Groves and Ravaged Gardens: The Fiction of Eudora Welty, Carson McCullers, and Flannery O'Connor.* Athens: University of Georgia Press, 1985. A comparative study that places Welty within the overlapping frames of southern and feminist literary traditions.

———. *Women Writers: Eudora Welty.* Totowa, N.J.: Barnes & Noble Books, 1989.

Weston, Ruth D. *Gothic Traditions and Narrative Techniques in the Fiction of Eudora Welty.* Baton Rouge: Louisiana State University Press, 1994.

INDEX